Message from South America

The Gold Cup goes to Uruguay . . . Waldemar Victorino scores the winner in their 2-1 victory over Brazil.

A JOURNEY which began at Heathrow Airport on Christmas Day 1980 may reach its logical conclusion in the Bernabeu Stadium in Madrid on 11 July, 1982. Because that is when I expect to see West Germany, Brazil or Argentina playing in the World Cup Final.

There weren't too many people inclined to give up their traditional Christmas at home in order to be in Montevideo for the 50th anniversary of the World Cup. But those of us who made the effort were rewarded with some dazzling football in bright sunshine, and with some useful pointers to what might happen in Spain.

One spectator with decidedly mixed feelings was the famous former Real Madrid centre half, Jose Santamaria. He was born in Uruguay and made his name there, so he could feel part of the host nation's celebrations when they won the Gold Cup. But he knows, as manager of Spain, just how much will be expected of him and his team now that they host the World Cup Finals.

Seven times out of 11, the host nation has reached the Final. Five times they have won it, including the last two World Cups in West Germany and Argentina.

So Santamaria and Spain will disappoint their public if they fail. And he knows only too well, having seen the standard of football he has to match, that their chances are not as good as, say, England's were in 1966.

Spanish football has been invaded from overseas by players brought in to boost club sides like Barcelona and Real Madrid. Despite the talent of home-produced stars, like goalkeeper Arconada, midfield man Zamora and forwards Juanito and Santillana, I think that Santamaria will do well to guide his team to the semi-finals.

And there, if what I saw in South America is any guide, they will be joined by Brazil, West Germany and the defending champions, Argentina. At the time of the Gold Cup, these were the best three teams in the world, and such care has been taken over their preparation since that I cannot see any one of them falling below that high standard now.

Argentina's manager, the handsome Cesar Luis Menotti, is in a privileged if vulnerable position. Privileged because he still has nine of his winning team from 1978 available; vulnerable because the champions are up there to be beaten, and so much is expected of the team who capitalised on the Latin atmosphere four years ago.

But there are two particular reasons why I think Menotti will take his side at least to the last four. Namely, Diego Maradona and Ramon Diaz.

These two products of the national youth team — Maradona, the world's most expensive player, and Diaz, the fastest centre forward in the game — have brought a new dimension to the Argentine side since 1978.

Maradona will be 21 when the World Cup Finals are played, Diaz a year older. Both will be considerably more experienced than Pele was when he inspired Brazil's World Cup victory in Europe in 1958. And both are that much the wiser as a result of playing in the Gold Cup.

In Uruguay, Maradona learned some home truths about the man-to-man marking which every team will use to stop him. And about keeping his temper when the temperature rises. Diaz scored a brilliant goal against the Germans — it ended Germany's run of 23 games without defeat — but he missed more chances than he took.

'Diaz is among the most exciting prospects we have ever produced in Argentina,' says Menotti. 'But he still has to learn how to balance himself properly when it comes to shooting. I spend a great deal of time with him in the training camp working on his finishing from various angles.'

In defence, Menotti is likely to rely on the experience of his stalwarts. Fillol is still an excellent goalkeeper, Passarella one of the finest players in the world and probably the best captain; Gallego's diligence in front of the back four is the reason the other midfield players can attack so freely.

'How do these South Americans get away with it when they push so many people forward?' asked the Tottenham manager, Keith Burkinshaw, when Oswaldo Ardiles came back from Uruguay. 'Because the individual defenders have so much pace, and are so comfortable with the ball, even near their own goal, that they can play their way out of trouble,' was the answer.

That is certainly true of Brazil, who have discovered a scintillating new centre back in Luisinho, and in left back Junior have acquired another expert when it comes to

DID YOU KNOW?

Trevor Brooking called them 'perhaps the best two goals I've ever scored' after his memorable twosome in last season's 4-0 win at home to Chelsea. His first was a 25-yard left-foot fizzer that scorched past Petar Borota's outstretched fingers . . . the second a right-footer that Brooking, out on West Ham's left, curled round the 'keeper and just inside the far post.

What did Borota think about them? 'They were two world-class goals — the best that have ever been put past me. I just stood and clapped as they went in'.

The triumphant Argentinians celebrate their 1978 World Cup victory.

Four good reaons why Argentina will be difficult to dethrone as World Cup holders . . . left, the magical Maradona; below, left, Passarella; below, centre, Fillol; and, below, right, the fastest centre-forward in the game, Diaz.

curling free kicks.

Their midfield includes two unfulfilled talents. Zico, regarded as the best player in Brazil, was disappointing in the last World Cup and is determined to make amends. Toninho Cerezo, the lanky, silky player alongside him, could be an even bigger revelation with his passing and forward runs.

A lot will depend on whether the Brazilians, now under the more adventurous management of Tele Santana, can find a natural goalscorer to finish off some of their embroidered attacking play.

I still have doubts about their captain and centre forward, Socrates, a qualified doctor, and wish that the tiny Reinaldo, so cruelly hit by knee injuries during his career, could fulfil the enormous promise he once showed.

Just to emphasise that Brazil want to play like their famous 1970 team, they have in their outside left, Ze Sergio, a cousin of the now retired Rivelino. His acceleration is one reason why wing play may again be in vogue in Spain.

It was certainly one reason why Uruguay (the host nation again, please note) won the Gold Cup in their own Centenario Stadium in Montevideo. They had a quicksilver outside right in 22-year-old Venacio Ramos, while the full backs, Hermes Moreira and Daniel Martinez, thundered forward in support. Significantly, they did not always attack down the touchline.

When I came back and told the Wolves coach, Richie Barker, how often the full backs popped up in the inside forward positions, he said: 'In world football now, there's a word called *underlapping*. Instead of making the extra man on the *outside,* which we call *overlapping,* the full back runs through a channel *inside* the defence. It could be something to watch out for in Spain.'

But my final message from the South America trip is strictly a European one. The West Germans, despite losing both Gold Cup matches and coming in for stern criticism from manager Jupp Derwall and their travelling press corps, did enough to convince many of us that they will be Europe's strongest card in the World Cup.

The European Champions have such strong, adaptable players with such high technical ability that nobody will relish being drawn against them. And the West German reputation for thoroughness and preparation means they will put in as much work with their squad as will Brazil and Argentina.

Karl-Heinz Rummenigge was out on his own among strikers in the Gold Cup.

Gold Cup finalists Brazil have the talent to mount another formidable challenge. Their stars include: left, Luisinho; right, their captain Socrates; below, left, Zico, regarded as the best player in Brazil, and below, right, Cerezo.

FUNSPOT

NICKNAME KNOW-HOW

Here are the jumbled-up nicknames of 25 well-known clubs in England and Scotland. First, solve the nickname, then give the name of the club:

1. STEFFEO .... (   )
2. ILSLIKE .... (   )
3. SABLED .... (   )
4. RAINSERM .... (   )
5. NEGRUNS .... (   )
6. LUBLY EWE .... (   )
7. RICHSEER .... (   )
8. SLIPMIRG .... (   )
9. SLAGEE .... (   )
10. EBES .... (   )
11. NEWMAILRAY .... (   )
12. PRUSS .... (   )
13. MARS .... (   )
14. RESTTORT .... (   )
15. REGS .... (   )
16. SPIM .... (   )
17. STATHER .... (   )
18. GASTS .... (   )
19. SHOP .... (   )
20. SNASW .... (   )
21. SNAGRICE .... (   )
22. HASKERS .... (   )
23. REQUASK .... (   )
24. ICENARAS .... (   )
25. DELSARDS .... (   )

Answers on page 77

Above: Uruguay line up for the Gold Cup Final. From left; back row — Rodriguez, Olivera, Krasowski, Martinez, Diogo, De Leon; front row — Ramos, De La Pena, Victorino, Paz, Morales. Right: Barrios, who went on as a substitute, celebrates after scoring Uruguay's first goal.

Hans-Pieter Briegel is becoming one of the most formidable defensive midfield players in the world and Karl-Heinz Forster at centre back is a compact, ruthless competitor.

West Germany's World Cup record is a pillar of consistency — winners twice (1954, 1974), runners-up once (1966), twice taking third place (1934, 1970) and once finishing fourth (1958). I fancy they will add to that record in 1982.

The British prospects for Spain will be mulled over many times in the next few months, but what is certain is that only a peak performance from one of the outsiders will resist the challenge of Maradona, Zico, Rummenigge and company.

And the main message from South America is still simply this: as long as we in England continue to put club before country, we will never compete with the elite of world football on level terms.

PERSONAL CHOICE

by John Motson

- **My teams as a boy** (and their stars):
  Chelsea — Jimmy Greaves, Peter Sillett; Charlton — Sam Bartram, Eddie Firmani.
- **Career background:**
  Born Salford. Educated Culford School, Bury St Edmunds. Joined Barnet Press (weekly newspaper), then Sheffield Morning Telegraph, then BBC's Radio 2 . . . then Match of the Day in 1971.
- **My first football assignment for BBC tv:**
  October, 1971: Liverpool 0, Everton 0. The match was utterly forgettable, the commentary even more so.
- **Club ground with best facilities for TV coverage:**
  Tottenham Hotspur. I have worked for the BBC in 22 countries; the commentary position at White Hart Lane is the best I have seen anywhere in the world.
- **Other sports I have commentated on:**
  Boxing and lawn tennis with regular radio commentating at Wimbledon for the last six years.
- **Most memorable soccer match I have covered:**
  Hereford 2, Newcastle 1 — FA Cup third round replay in 1972. It was my first Cup match for BBC tv and one of my close friends, Ricky George, scored the winning goal.
- **My kind of football reading:**
  I read every football book, paper and magazine I can get my hands on, at home or abroad. My favourite writers are Jeff Powell *(Daily Mail)* and Mike Langley *(Sunday People)*. French magazines *Onze* and *France Football* are the best I have seen.
- **Change in the game I would like to see:**
  The First Division reduced to 16 clubs, to give us more time in the season for the England team to get together.
- **Most exciting players in Britain today:**
  Trevor Francis, his speed and finishing are essential to the England team. Glenn Hoddle — he's the best two-footed player and has the most vision. Kevin Keegan — his attitude is an example to all.
- **The match I wish I could have covered:**
  The 1950 World Cup Final between Brazil and Uruguay. I have been to the Maracana Stadium twice since, and would love to have been there when they had the world record crowd of 200,000 for that match.
- **Among my souvenirs:**
  A Brazilian shirt from the 1974 World Cup; the referee's whistle from the first match I covered (referee John Yates); a signed artist's impression of Mick Mills, the player I most admire.
- **My biggest broadcasting gaff:**
  Telling viewers: 'For the benefit of those watching in black and white, Spurs are wearing the yellow shirts.'
- **Moment of magic I'll never forget:**
  Nelinho's goal for Brazil in the 1978 World Cup third-place match against Italy.
- **Manager I admire most:**
  Keith Burkinshaw (Tottenham), because he is the most honest person I have met in football.
- **Personality of the past I would like to have interviewed:**
  Arsenal's Herbert Chapman. He must have been 50 years ahead of his time.
- **Strangest incident I've seen on a football field:**
  In a Derby v Manchester City match, when they had to paint the penalty spot before they could take the kick.
- **I'd give him a medal:**
  Every manager and secretary in the Fourth Division. Keeping the game going at that level is the hardest job in the business.
- **The man I would like to see manage England when Ron Greenwood retires:**
  Bobby Robson — his record at Ipswich speaks for itself — or Brian Clough, coupled with Peter Taylor — their record is the best in football.
- **The man I think will get the job when Ron Greenwood retires:**
  Bobby Robson.
- **1982 World Cup winners:**
  West Germany or Brazil. They both impressed me enormously when I went to Uruguay to watch the Gold Cup tournament last January.

PERSONAL CHOICE

HALL OF FAME · HALL OF FAME · HALL OF FAME · HALL OF FAME · HALL OF FAME

STEVE MORAN, Southampton's 20-year-old striker, made a stunning impact last season. *Match of the Day* cameras saw him score against Manchester City on his debut as substitute in January 1980 — and he took the First Division by storm with 16 goals in his first 18 matches in 1980-1. Saints manager Lawrie McMenemy spotted him as a schoolboy playing Sunday-morning football. Noting the skill and worn-out boots, he offered him a new pair if he scored a hat-trick. Steve obliged . . . and never looked back.

HALL OF FAME · HALL OF FAME · HALL OF FAME · HALL OF FAME

GRAHAM RIX, of Arsenal, had good reason to remember last season. He took over Arsenal's main midfield role following the departure of Liam Brady to Juventus and won full England recognition from Ron Greenwood in six of the ten Internationals in 1980-1. Born at Doncaster, he joined Arsenal from school, scored on his debut against Leicester as a 19-year-old in 1977 and quickly graduated to England Under-21 and 'B' team honours. He played in Arsenal's three successive FA Cup Finals in 1978-79-80.

HALL OF FAME · HALL OF FAME · HALL OF FAME · HALL OF FAME · HALL OF FAME

STEVE ARCHIBALD, of Tottenham, strong-running, hard-shooting central striker, was described by Aberdeen manager Alex Ferguson as 'the finest player to emerge from Scotland since Kenny Dalglish' when he transferred him to Spurs in May 1980 for £830,000. Originally with Clyde, Steve justified that opinion with a prolific first season for Spurs, finishing 1980-1 with an FA Cup Winner's medal in the 100th Final and the season's Golden Shoe award as the top First Division scorer with 25 goals.

HALL OF FAME · HALL OF FAME · HALL OF FAME · HALL OF FAME

GARY OWEN, of WBA, is the player Malcolm Allison said he most regretted transferring during his time as Manchester City manager. He had taken this son of a local Rugby League player to Maine Road as a 14-year-old, and Gary went into City's first team at 18, making immediate impact in the centre of midfield. He was signed by Ron Atkinson for West Bromwich in May 1979 for £450,000 and subsequently captained the England Under-21 side.

FIRST PHASE (13 June-25 June)

Groups	Countries	Venues	Stadia	Time	Days														Groups	
					1	2	3	4	5	6	7	8	9	10	11	12	13	14		
					Sun	Mon	Tue	Wed	Thu	Fri	Sat	Sun	Mon	Tue	Wed	Thu	Fri	Sat		
6	24	12	13	2	13	14	15	16	17	18	19	20	21	22	23	24	25	26	1	2
1	1	Vigo	Balaidos	1		1-2				1-3					1-4				A1	C7
	2			2																
	3	Coruna	Riazor	1			3-4				2-4			3-2						
	4			2																
2	5	Gijon	El Molinon	1				5-6				5-7					5-8		B4	D10
	6			2																
	7	Oviedo	Carlos Tartiere	1					7-8				6-8			6-7				
	8			2																
3	9	Alicante	J. Rico Perez	1	*														A3	C9
	10			2	9-10					9-11					9-12					
	11	Elche	Nuevo Estadio	1																
	12			2			11-12				10-12			10-11						
4	13	Bilbao	San Mames	1				13-14				13-15					13-16		B6	D12
	14			2																
	15	Valladolid	Nuevo Estadio	1					15-16				14-16			14-15				
	16			2																
5	17	Valencia	Luis Casanova	1															D11	B5
	18			2				17-18				17-19					17-20			
	19	Zaragoza	La Romareda	1																
	20			2					19-20				18-20			18-19				
6	21	Sevilla	Villamarin S. Pizjuan	1															C8	A2
	22			2		21-22				21-23					21-24					
	23	Malaga	La Rosaleda	1																
	24			2			23-24				22-24			22-23						

Covering the World

Alec Weeks, Executive Producer of Sport,

talks to Albert Sewell, Match of the Day Researcher and Statistician

BY THE TIME the starting whistle blows at the opening match next June, Alec Weeks will be on 1982 World Cup duty in Spain for the 12th time. As BBCtv's Executive Producer of all major sporting events, he made his first planning visit before any of the Home Countries had begun their qualifying programme.

Those multi-purpose reconnaissance trips, taking him to the 17 stadia in the 14 Spanish cities and towns where the World Cup will be staged, have been made at regular intervals over the past two years. The homework actually began at the last world series in Argentina four years ago.

Alec has been checking on accommodation for the 60-65 personnel who will be involved in the BBC's presentation of this 12th World Cup; assessing camera positions and interview facilities at all the grounds; looking at communications between the venues; and liaising with Spanish TV heads and programme directors who will be responsible for all the actual match coverage during the most concentrated month of football action in the game's history.

SECOND PHASE (28 June-5 July)

Groups	Countries	Venues	Stadia	Days										Semi Finalists
				15	16	17	18	19	20	21	22	23	24	
				Sun	Mon	Tue	Wed	Thu	Fri	Sat	Sun	Mon	Tue	
4	12	2	4	27	28	29	30	1	2	3	4	5	6	
A	1 2 3	Barcelona	Nou Camp		1 3			1 2			2 3			A
B	4 5 6	Madrid	Santiago Bernabeu			4 6			4 5			5 6		B
C	7 8 9	Barcelona	Sarria			7 9			7 8			8 9		C
D	10 11 12	Madrid	Vicente Calderon		10 12			10 11			11 12			D

SEMI-FINALS

Countries	Venues	Stadia	Days		
			25	26	27
			Wed	Thu	Fri
			7	8	9
A C	Barcelona	Nou Camp		A C	
B D	Sevilla	Sanchez Pizjuan		B D	

FINALS

Countries	Venues	Stadia	Days	
			28	29
			Sat	Sun
			10	11
Losers	Alicante	Rico Perez	3v4	
Winners	Madrid	Santiago Bernabeu		FINAL

WORLD CUP 82

Insert the names of the countries competing in Spain when the draw is made on 16 January 1982

*Opening match, featuring the World Cup holders Argentina, will be played at the Nou Camp Stadium, Barcelona on 13 June.

1	
2	
3	
4	
5	
6	
7	
8	
9	*Argentina
10	
11	
12	
13	
14	
15	
16	
17	Spain
18	
19	
20	
21	
22	
23	
24	

Cup, the BBC way

Since joining BBCtv as an office boy in 1941, Alec Weeks has come all the way up the ranks to Executive Producer. He was Senior Producer at the last four World Cup tournaments, a role that will be filled in Spain by Fred Viner, his successor last season as *Match of the Day* Series Producer.

This is how Alec sees the most complicated, competitive and costly World Cup operation unfolding in Spain:

‘In every possible way, this is going to be the biggest tournament ever staged — on the field and on the screen. There are 24 countries this time instead of 16 . . . 52 matches instead of 36, spanning a full month instead of three weeks.

The last World Cup, in Argentina, was played at only six venues. Now there will be 17, with three centres (Madrid, Barcelona and Seville) each providing two grounds.

All those scattered venues will present the media with the greatest communications challenge it has ever faced. The match pictures you see on your screen will be shot by Spanish Television. Our own camera crews will provide all the material for our day-by-day back-up coverage — stories and interviews from the training camps and so on.

From each of the six qualifying groups, the top two will go forward to play in four sections of three. From these will come the four semi-finalists, with the two losers

Alec Weeks . . . behind him, on his office wall, are maps of Spain and a World Cup chart.

playing off for third and fourth place and the two winners contesting the grand finale in Madrid's Bernabeau Stadium on 11 July.

Our coverage will be what I call a "BBC United" operation, with up to 65 personnel out there and another 40 working at the actual transmission end in London. All the match coverage and day-by-day film stories will be channelled to London via the big new Spanish TV centre in Madrid.

Our front men, of course, are the commentary and reporting teams, backed up by the best technicians and cameramen drawn from London and the BBC regions. Main network coverage and "opt-outs" (ie, special features on our other countries playing in Spain) will all be packaged through to TV Centre in London from our operations room in Madrid.

The first round matches, spread over a dozen venues, will present the biggest problems to Spanish TV and ourselves. After that, the geography will be concentrated on fewer centres.

From January onwards, each ground will be given its final facelift. They can leave it as late as that in Spain, because there is no midwinter hold-up through the weather.

At the start of the planning operation, we allowed for up to four of our countries qualifying. It could, of course, be fewer — or five, counting the Republic of Ireland as "one of us".

Our four commentary teams will need to be highly mobile, especially during the first round, shifting quickly from match to match. Getting them from venue to venue will be an operation in itself, but we'll be there!

DID YOU KNOW?

Charlton Athletic are the only club to reach the FA Cup Final after losing a match on the way to Wembley. It happened in 1945-6, first season of the competition after the war. For the only time, the Cup was played on a home-and-away basis until the semi-finals and in the third round Charlton lost the away fixture by 2-1 at Fulham. But they won the home leg 3-1 and took the tie 4-3 on aggregate. They went all the way to Wembley, where Derby County beat them 4-1 in the Final.

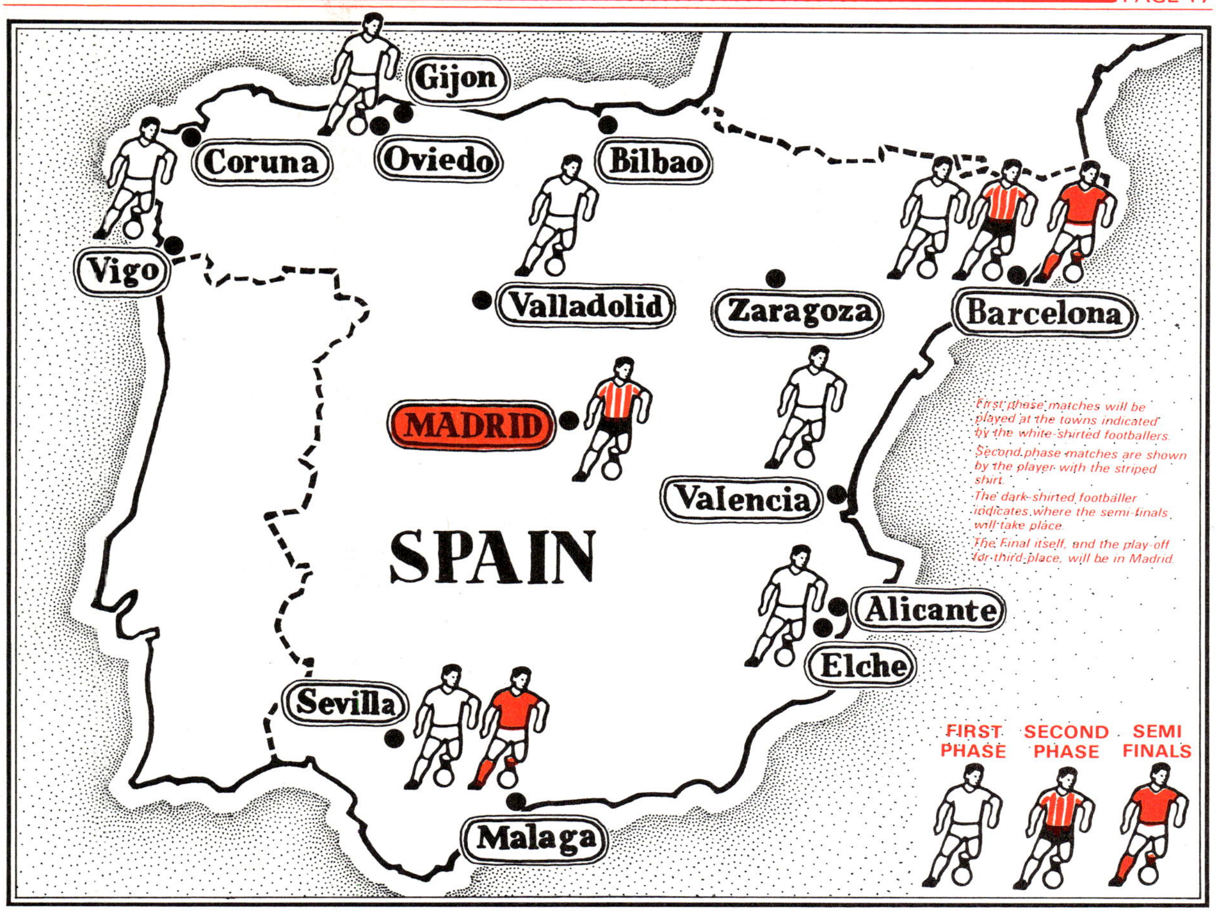

Venues for the 1982 World Cup. The Final takes place in Madrid.

Kick-off times will be at 4.15pm BST at the grounds in Northern Spain, and at 8pm in Madrid and the South, where it will be so much hotter. The inaugural match and the Final are scheduled for 7pm.

Spanish TV will cover every match in colour. They are setting up 20 outside broadcast units, with seven cameras in use at each game — four in the usual positions, two isolated and high-up, one at low level. BBC will have coverage of *every* match, live or recorded.

How much, or how little, we show of some of the smaller matches in the first round will be decided on the spot. Who is to say, in advance, what one or more of the "little countries" might achieve, remembering the exciting contribution the North Koreans made when the World Cup was held in England? ❜

That 1966 tournament really put the World Cup on the map in terms of television coverage. It has grown at every competition since.

Before the last World Cup in Argentina, Alec Weeks was the special guest at a seminar held in Buenos Aires, and talked to 120 TV directors, producers, cameramen on how to get the best possible effect from their match coverage. He was a little sceptical.

But, give or take a few snags in the early stages, he was impressed by the way the 1978 tournament was covered. After one important first-round match, he went to the 'scanner' and said to the sweating Argentine TV director: 'Well done, you deserve a "thank you" from every country in the world where these pictures have been seen tonight.' The reply gave Alec one of his proudest moments: 'Thank *you,* sir. We covered it the way you said — the BBC way.'

During the past summer, Alec addressed a similar seminar in Madrid, helping Spain's top TV men prepare the intricate presentation of the 1982 World Cup. 'We are glad to give any help we can,' says Alec.

A new Spanish Government has meant new heads of department, new policies, new people coming into the World Cup discussions. Alec reflects: 'Every World Cup has had its anxieties, its excitement, its satisfaction. I look back on them all with enjoyment and am looking forward to Spain

TOP MEN BEHIND OUR WORLD CUP COVERAGE IN SPAIN

LINKED by headphones and microphone to his commentator and cameramen, **Fred Viner,** BBCtv's Executive Producer of Association Football, sits in his cramped capsule known as the scanner, surveys a bank of up to ten monitors, each offering a different 'shot' and, at the press of a button at his complicated control panel, selects the *Match of the Day* pictures that appear on your screen at home. That is the basic description of an extremely complex operation.

Fred's youthful ambition to become a professional footballer led to his being on the books of his local club, Norwich City but at 18 his career changed course as he moved to BBC Radio on the engineering side.

He joined BBCtv in 1955, became chief sub-editor in the newsroom at Alexandra Palace, then editorial producer of TV news, writing scripts to film and video-tape. When a cameraman went sick one day, Fred did the job, was at once hooked on outside coverage and spent the next six years as a film cameraman.

In 1964 he found himself working a video-tape shift at the Tokio Olympic Games and was subsequently appointed joint producer, with Ricky Tilling, of *Sportsview* and *Grandstand,* alternating a month at a time on each programme.

Fred edited the first *Match of the Day* in 1964, then switched to directing outside broadcasts, with the Grand National and Wimbledon tennis his 'specialities'.

As director-producer, Fred handled the Wimbledon Centenary final in 1977, the 200th running of the Derby in 1979 and, last season, the 100th FA Cup Final and its magnificent replay.

WHAT **Bob Abrahams** does not know about the technical and editorial presentation of football on television would fill rather less than the back of a Cup Final ticket stub. After producing *Football Focus* for the last two years, he was appointed Editor of *Match of the Day* last June, 23 years after he joined the BBC from the feature film industry.

Bob, London-born at Hoxton, grew up with football in his blood. From 1946 his team were — and still are — Spurs. The football they played, first under Arthur Rowe and then Bill Nicholson, gave him an appreciation of quality that has remained his yardstick. And his eyes glinted once more at the style of their 100th FA Cup Final triumph last May.

When he first came to the BBC, Bob worked on *Sportsview* with Paul Fox and, after two breaks away from sport, during which his talents were applied to the *Panorama* and *Tonight* programmes, he concentrated on football.

One of his proudest productions was the coaching film, featuring tactics and skills, which he made in conjunction with the Football Association. From first shooting until screening last Christmas, it took a year to complete.

As Editor of the BBC's biggest sports coverage operation, Bob Abrahams will back the World Cup commentating and reporting teams with a knowledge of pictures, words and football presentation that is second to none.

And in Spain, or anywhere else for that matter, anyone who would dare to suggest within his hearing that football is not *the* greatest game ever devised can expect the argument of a lifetime from the little man with an unquenchable enthusiasm and love for soccer.

with keener anticipation than ever.

'I hope our countries do us proud on the field and give the millions of viewers at home something special. It's time we played a part again in the greatest football show on earth.

'Frankly, at this stage, I'm wondering just a little what sort of pictures we might get from Spanish TV at some of the early matches. But, then, I've worried about the same thing before every World Cup. It wouldn't be me if I didn't.

'Perhaps I should be concerned about how they might cover the Final, because their cameramen can get so emotional. At a crucial moment in one of Spain's matches, I once saw them drop their hands in the excitement, and for a few moments the pictures went haywire. If Spain get to the Final on 11 July, anything could happen.'

Viewing figures for the last World Cup

Research figures for live coverage of the 1978 World Cup matches in Argentina showed that BBC had a total audience of 221.9 million viewers and ITV 146.7 million viewers:—

	BBC	*ITV*
First Round (14 matches)	145m	77.4m
Second Round (4 matches)	45.7m	53.7m
Third Place Match	11.6m	5.8m
Final	19.6m	9.8m
Total:	221.9m	146.7m

FUNSPOT

DIAL-A-STAR

Hidden in our Match of the Day telephone are the names of two top stars, spelt out every second letter. Can you find them?

Answers on page 77

Win a trip to the World Cup

IT'S a football fan's dream come true — an all-expenses-paid trip to Spain to see the World Cup match of your choice. It could be one of the early games to ensure that you see your favourite team among the qualifiers — or it could be the World Cup Final itself.

Match of the Day Annual offers you this once-in-a-lifetime opportunity. We'll fly you out to Spain the day before the match and back the day after, with hotel accommodation arranged for two nights. To make sure that everything goes smoothly on your World Cup adventure, you'll be accompanied by a BBC representative.

To win this exciting trip, you must answer correctly the six questions listed below and then say, in not more than 25 words, why you would like to see a World Cup match as guest of the BBC. There will also be six runners-up who will each receive a football specially autographed by Kevin Keegan. The winner and runners-up will be chosen by Jimmy Hill, the Editor of *Match of the Day* and the Editor of *Match of the Day* Annual. The name of the winner will be announced on *Match of the Day* during March 1982. The runners-up will be notified by post. The decision is final and binding and no correspondence will be entered into.

To enter our competition you must be 16 years old or younger. You may only enter once. You must not work for the BBC or be related to anyone employed by the BBC. The competition is open only to residents of the United Kingdom and the Republic of Ireland. Closing date is 31 January 1982.

Now for the six questions:

1. Holders (Argentina) and hosts (Spain) apart, which was the first country to qualify for the 1982 World Cup in Spain?

2. Six different countries have won the World Cup. Who are they?

3. What is the name of Spain's little-boy symbol for the 1982 World Cup — he's shaped like an orange, is wearing football kit and holding a ball?

4. Only one country has appeared in the Final series of all previous 11 World Cup competitions. Name, please?

5. What is England's biggest win in a World Cup match?

6. In which years did (a) England, (b) N. Ireland, (c) Scotland, (d) Wales last participate in the World Cup Final series?

List your answers on a postcard and write your words about the World Cup beginning with the phrase: **I would like to see a World Cup match in Spain because . . .** Add your name, age and address and then post to:

World Cup Competition, Room G.065, BBC Kensinton House, Richmond Way, Shepherd's Bush, London W14 0AX.

Win a trip to the World Cup

Win a trip to the World Cup

Win a trip to the World Cup

I'M BACKING THESE BLACK ACES

Dave Bennett . . . excellent control and vision

says Jimmy Hill

THE PRESENCE of black players in our game has been felt for some time and, as the years have gone on, they have made, and are making, an increasing impact. There are now few clubs who do not have a coloured lad on their pay-roll and many black players have earned international recognition at different levels.

It is good that we are able to field black players in our national teams because they bring an added physical dimension to the game. They often possess outstanding pace, and are not lacking when it comes to winning the ball in the air. In addition, they seem to be able to acquire ball skills very readily.

Watching Cyrille Regis, Viv Anderson or Garth Crooks, you cannot fail to notice their graceful movement and a feeling of potential power.

A good measure of their ever-increasing place in our game was the 1981 FA Cup Final, in which three players entertained us in vastly different ways — Chris Hughton in defence and Garth Crooks and Dave Bennett up front.

I nicknamed Dave Bennett the *Black Ghost* because he was extremely effective for Manchester City in an unobtrusive way. He has good control, excellent vision and a very gentle and accurate touch when he's laying the ball off. It is seldom that a movement breaks down on him and he achieves it all without flamboyance.

In that way he is different from Garth Crooks, who is equally skilful but far more expressive in the way he contributes to the game. He is older than Bennett and has taken time to develop into such an effective all-round player. I remember, when he began with Stoke, he was a nervous and weak finisher but now he relishes the responsibility of putting the ball in the net. The enjoyment he got from scoring for Spurs at Wembley was there for all to see.

Viv Anderson and Laurie Cunningham . . . England caps have rewarded their skills.

Chris Hughton, Tottenham's left-back, qualifies for the Republic of Ireland on the basis that his mother was born in Limerick. Chris himself was born at Forest Gate, in East London, and his father was from Guyana but he opted to play for the Republic rather than wait to see if England selected him. From what I've seen of him, I reckon that had he been patient he would have been good enough to win England honours. Instead, he may well set a new Irish record for the number of caps he wins.

It is England full-back Viv Anderson's extreme pace that makes him a formidable opponent in defence and such a threat in overlapping positions. He flew the flag and became the first coloured player to represent England in a full international when he played at Wembley against Czechoslovakia in November 1977.

Another coloured back, West Bromwich Albion's Brendon Batson, relies on anticipation and calculation to rob opponents, rather than on sheer speed. I noticed, too, the performance of young Chris Ramsey, of Brighton, in their nerve-racking relegation struggle last season and he certainly didn't let them down.

I have high hopes that Danny Thomas, Coventry's right-back and midfield player, will follow in Anderson's footsteps in the years to come. Danny made a good start by being selected for England's Under-21 side against the Republic of Ireland last February.

Vince Hilaire, in the role of midfield-winger, is another coloured player to catch the eye and was rewarded with Under-21 honours again last season. It certainly wasn't his fault that Crystal Palace were relegated.

Up to now, we have seen few black goalkeepers in Britain but Manchester City have a young man named Alex Williams waiting for Joe Corrigan to come down from the extraordinarily high pedestal he has

Garth Crooks . . . skill and power make him a potent, confident goalscorer.

occupied for so long. Judging from the way Joe played in the 1981 Cup Final, that may not be for some time yet.

There are plenty of black central defenders around the League — George Berry (Wolverhampton Wanderers), Bob Hazell (Queens Park Rangers) and Pedro Richards, of Notts County, to name but three. Berry also chose to play for the country of his mother, Wales, although he was born in West Germany, where his father was serving with the British Army.

Of course, in midfield, wing and striking positions, black players have a better chance of expressing their individual ability and Remi Moses, of West Bromwich Albion, combines endeavour on the ball with dour, defensive qualities and an abundance of stamina.

If there is an overall criticism that could be made of black players, it is that they tend to flash in and out of the game rather than contribute over the 90 minutes — but Moses is an absolute dynamo.

Luton are well served by Brian Stein's attacking qualities — he was their top scorer last season with 20 goals — and Ricky Hill is a player who has interested me from the time Eric Morecambe, then a Luton director, confided to me that he had watched him, at the age of 16, perform astonishing feats of skill. What I have seen of him confirms Eric's view. One of the reasons I wanted Luton to win promotion to the First Division was to see how Ricky Hill would measure up in top company.

I suppose tall, black No. 9s make us sit up and take notice of coloured players more than any others. They are big men, it's true, but seldom clumsy or short of good control of the ball and they bring something extra to what used to be called centre-forward play. Cyrille Regis, of West Bromwich Albion, Justin Fashanu, of Norwich, and Garry Thompson, of Coventry, are all powerfully built, physical, fast and skilful and have an eye for a goal chance, however slight.

Cyrille Regis and Justin Fashanu . . . goalscorers with the golden touch.

If that batch isn't enough to open your eyes, you may care to note a number of young players ready to step into their shoes, like Terry Connor, of Leeds, Paul Davis, of Arsenal, Bobby Barnes, of West Ham, and Howard Gayle, the card Liverpool manager Bob Paisley kept up his sleeve until he played him to bemuse Bayern Munich in last season's European Cup semi-final.

It's impossible to write on this subject without mentioning Laurie Cunningham, now with Real Madrid, and one of the first black players I noted on account of his extraordinary acceleration. He used to devastate full-backs by pushing the ball past them and destroy them by sheer pace but when I've seen him more recently, and particularly on his few performances for England, he seemed content to run inside, which I think makes him far less dangerous.

Unless he learns to play to his strength again, it is unlikely that he will make further progress in the game; not for England, anyway. It's strange that while opposing full-backs remain fearful of Cunningham's pace, he neglects to use his most powerful asset against them.

Not all the coloured stars are with big clubs. For example, the leading black marksman in the Football League is Joe Cooke who had a career total of 80 goals with Bradford City, Peterborough and Oxford United before joining Exeter last June.

As the years go on, I expect to see black footballers make an increasing impact on the game. They are numerous enough already for the novelty to have worn off, which can only be a good thing. Happily, the nasty racial taunts which used to come from some spectators are on the decrease.

So we should rejoice that the black player has come to stay in this country because he makes our club sides and our international teams more exciting, entertaining and successful. I just wonder who's going to be the first black manager?

PERSONAL CHOICE

by Jimmy Hill

My team as a boy:
Fulham. My Dad took me — they were his team, too. My Saturday heroes were full-backs Joe Bacuzzi and Mike Keeping and when I went to Craven Cottage as a young pro I felt honoured to play in the same side as men like Joe and Jim Taylor.

Career background:
I played for Reading's 'A' team (Ted Drake was manager there at the time), signed professional for Brentford and within two months was in their Second Division side, wearing No 9. Then I moved to Fulham and, finally, back to Brentford before a cartilage injury finished my playing career in 1961. From 1957-61 I was Chairman of the Players' Union (now the PFA) and became manager of Coventry City in November 1961. I first got a foot into TV when doing interviews on behalf of the Players' Union and was called in to do a linking job for ITV in London on the night of the Manchester United air crash in February 1958. I left Coventry in October 1967, six months after they got into the First Division for the first time, basically because they wouldn't give me a ten-year contract. Then the job of Head of Sport and football presenter on London Weekend came along — I had five seasons with *The Big Match* — and in 1972 the BBC made me the offer to front *Match of the Day*.

Most memorable match I have covered:
The 1966 World Cup Final with the BBC, as a 'guest' while managing Coventry. Joe Mercer was alongside me and, after England had won the Final, it suddenly sank in that we were World Champions — and we both cried our eyes out!

Changes in the game I would like to see:
I think most viewers know my feelings about the cynical foul. I'd like to restrict the amount of time goalkeepers can waste with the ball in their hands by, somehow, making it 'too hot to handle'. And I think the 35-yard offside area that the Americans have introduced over there (instead of half the pitch) would be good for the game all over the world.

The match I wish I could have covered:
It hasn't been played yet — the next time England win the World Cup.

Among my souvenirs:
I cherish most the cuttings books that my Dad kept of just about everything that appeared about me from the time I came into the game as a young professional.

Moments of magic I'll never forget:
Pele jumping to take the ball on his chest, then scoring a marvellous World Cup goal for Brazil. And some of Bobby Charlton's breathtaking runs and brilliant shooting.

Managers I most admire:
I'm full of admiration for the fellows who do a marvellous bricks-without-straw job, like two of the 'moderns' George Kerr, of Grimsby, and Alan Mullery for Brighton.

Personality of the past I would like to have interviewed:
Alex James, in the pre-war glory days of Arsenal. When I was a kid, his was the football name on everyone's lips.

Craziest match I have ever seen:
I not only saw it . . . I played in it. Fulham, of course! We were at Plymouth and our 'keeper, Frank Elliott, won the ball well at an opponent's feet, then rolled over — and threw the ball into his own net. Soon after, Frank went off injured. Winger Charlie Mitten took the jersey and with ten men (no subs in those days) and a makeshift 'keeper, we were stronger! Then Frank returned . . . and we went 2-1 down. So Charlie took over in goal again . . . and we drew level, only for Plymouth to beat us 3-2 with a last-minute goal. If only we'd had it on *Match of the Day*!

My biggest surprise at a match:
Going to Highbury for Arsenal v Liverpool, in my London Weekend days, and finishing up 'on the line'. One of the linesmen pulled a muscle and the game was held up while an appeal was made over the public address for someone qualified to take his place. After five minutes nothing had happened, the crowd were chi-hiking and I could see *The Big Match* becoming *The Abandoned Match*. So I rushed down from the stand to see if I could help (it was as well I'd taken a referee's course as a player). It turned out that I was the only qualified 'applicant' under about 60 and when referee Pat Partridge saw me, he said: 'You'll do Jim. Get changed . . . and make it quick.' That experience, in front of a 40,000 crowd, made me acutely aware of the responsibilities referees and linesmen have.

1982 World Cup winners:
West Germany — they've done an excellent team rebuilding job — or Spain. Host countries have a great record in the World Cup.

PERSONAL CHOICE

1980/81 Roll of Honour

League Champions:
Aston Villa

FA Cup:
Tottenham Hotspur

League Cup:
Liverpool

Scottish League Champions:
Celtic

Scottish FA Cup:
Rangers

Scottish League Cup:
Dundee Utd.

European Cup:
Liverpool

European Cup-winners Liverpool returned home to a rapturous reception from 500,000 people. Manager Bob Paisley holds the trophy for all to see.

European Cup Winners' Cup
Dynamo Tbilisi

UEFA Cup:
Ipswich Town

CROSSWORD

COMPILED BY JOHN WEATHERHEAD

CLUES

Across

1. Albion watched from the Pavilion (8,3,4)
8. St. James's Alan used fairly in charge (8)
9. Garth supporting the shepherds (6)
11. Oriental forerunner of Fife and Stirling (4)
12. The cost of Match of the Day? (7,3)
13. Normally it introduced Waring on Grandstand (5)
15. TV frames for prefects? (8)
19. Field placing is reversed in potion (8)
20. Sharp if close games rest on its edge (5)
23. Ex-Yorks division of Leeds, Huddersfield etc? (4,6)
25. Low joint disabling cartilagenous drop-outs (4)
27. TV Panel's drink when Villa meet Hammers? (6)
28. Park loyalist on the Wear (8)
29. Cheerful doughboys of Rotherham (3,5,7)

Down

1. Titles favoured by some managers and unions (6)
2. Civil War stalwarts of Somerton Park (9)
3. Following Jimmy, he rises to Match of the Day (4)
4. Commentator's words as opening goal is scored (3,3)
5. Way to goal maybe if I credit no confusion (9)
6. Armchair switch for missing opponents' goals? (2-3)
7. Terrace taunt, not doubly difficult, for team outclassed (4,4)
10. Shireless county of Upton Park's Alan (5)
14. If you don't do it with play, you're not offside (9)
16. United attack on goal in a vulgar manner? (9)
17. Robson's greats on a short tee (7,1)
18. Billy, a premium investment of Lyall and GPO (5)
21. Playing well — astride bench it seems (2,4)
22. Martin of '66 World Cup fame (6)
24. Neil Armstrong's advice to find it on the field? (5)
26. McMenemy's valley! (4)

(Answers on page 77)

JOE JORDAN, of Manchester United, one of the Old Trafford stars hit by injury last season, quickly set about making up for a ten-match absence and became top scorer again with 15 goals. He began with Morton, moving to Leeds United in October 1970 (£15,000). By the time he joined Manchester United in January 1978 his value had risen to £350,000, then a record for the club. He won his first Scotland cap against England in 1973 and at the start of this season had represented his country 47 times.

DENNIS MORTIMER's inspiring leadership was a significant factor in Aston Villa's League Championship triumph last season. Villa's 28-year-old captain and midfield star joined them from Coventry in December 1975 (£175,000) and at the start of 1981-2 was approaching a total of 400 League appearances for his two clubs. He comes from Liverpool and was a centre-back when capped by England Youth and Under-23s. He captained England 'B' last season and was a strong contender for full honours.

PAUL POWER, of Manchester City, is one of football's 'local boys who made good'. He decided to further his education rather than plunge into the professional game and remained an amateur while studying law at university. Eventually, this left-sided midfield player signed professional in July 1975 and he contributed to the club's big revival last season. He captained City to the 100th FA Cup Final, scoring five goals on the way to Wembley.

ALAN HANSEN, tall and stylish, became a first-choice central defender for Liverpool after Emlyn Hughes moved to Wolves. He also established a place in Scotland's back four He moved from Partick Thistle to Anfield in a £100,000 transfer in May 1977 and has developed a most effective defensive partnership alongside England's Phil Thompson. He shot the goal that beat West Ham in the 1981 League Cup Final replay.

	P	W	D	L	F	A	Pts
Championship	22	18	4	0	74	15	40
F. A. Cup	5	5	0	0	11	0	-

Proud Preston North End . . . in 1888-9 they became the first side to do the 'double'.

The "double" that gets

by Bob Wilson (one of the few players who have achieved it)

THERE can't be anybody in British football who wasn't pleased when Ipswich Town won the UEFA Cup. At the end of a season when they were threatening to win everything and came alarmingly close to finishing with nothing, it would have been the roughest of justice had they failed to get their hands on one trophy.

Not many people outside the immediate vicinity of Aston Villa's famous ground would dispute the assertion that Ipswich were just about the most attractive team in England last season.

The pure quality of their football gave them a head start on most and they looked to have a squad of players whose numbers and versatility could take care of any injury emergency.

I know Aston Villa won the League title. I also know that Ipswich lost it — and with it the chance to become only the fifth club to achieve the domestic double of League title and FA Cup.

Preston did it in 1888-9. Aston Villa followed suit in 1896-7. After 64 years, Tottenham were there in 1960-1 — and I was a member of the Arsenal side that climbed soccer's Everest in 1970-1.

The 'double' gets harder all the time.

Preston's feat was achieved in the League's opening season. They won the 12-club championship without losing a match and the FA Cup without conceding a goal. This was their record:

Eight years later . . . and it's Aston Villa's turn to parade with the two trophies.

harder all the time

PRESTON N.E. 1888-9

	P	W	D	L	F	A	Pts
Championship	22	18	4	0	74	15	40
FA Cup	5	5	0	0	11	0	—
	27	23	4	0	85	15	—

When Aston Villa emulated Preston in 1896-7, a Second Division had been added to the League and the First Division had grown to 16 clubs. Like Preston before them, Villa took the League title by an 11-points margin; they needed only 37 matches to win both trophies. This was their record:

ASTON VILLA 1896-7

	P	W	D	L	F	A	Pts
Championship	30	21	5	4	73	38	47
FA Cup	7	5	2	0	17	7	—
	37	26	7	4	90	45	—

The League increased in numbers. Competition became sharper. The myth grew that the double was an impossible dream.

Then manager Bill Nicholson, skipper Danny Blanchflower and their magnificent Tottenham team won their first 11 League matches in 1960-1 and had the Championship fairly safely locked up before they began their Cup conquest.

When Spurs went into their FA Cup semi-final against Burnley, they led the table by four points from Sheffield Wednesday, with a game in hand. At the finish, with a total of 115 goals, they won the Championship by eight points and at Wembley beat Leicester 2-0 to complete the double in 49 matches. This was their record, with no involvement in Europe:

TOTTENHAM HOTSPUR 1960-1

	P	W	D	L	F	A	Pts
Championship	42	31	4	7	115	55	66
FA Cup	7	6	1	0	21	4	—
	49	37	5	7	136	59	—

Leeds United, in 1969-70, were the next club to make a bold bid for the double, as part

TOTTENHAM HOTSPUR 1960-61

	P	W	D	L	F	A	Pts
Championship	42	31	4	7	115	55	66
F.A. Cup	7	6	1	0	21	4	-

In 1960-1 Tottenham became the first team this century to achieve 'the impossible'.

of a treble with the European Cup as their third target. On the day that Leeds played Manchester United in the semi-final of the FA Cup, they were second in the Championship, three points behind the leaders, Everton, with a game in hand. A European Cup semi-final against Celtic lay ahead.

Two drawn FA Cup semi-finals against Manchester United added to the pressure. At the third attempt, Leeds reached the final but Celtic knocked them out of the European Cup 3-1 on aggregate. At Wembley, Leeds twice forfeited the lead in the FA Cup Final against Chelsea, who won the replay 2-1 at Old Trafford. Everton strode away with the Championship — and a season that offered Leeds three prizes late in March ended with them empty-handed.

Twelve months later came the most memorable season of my life. When we met Stoke in the FA Cup semi-final, Arsenal were third in the table, six points behind the leaders, Leeds, but with three games in hand. Four days earlier we went out of the Fairs Cup, defeated on away goals by Cologne at the quarter-final stage. We beat Stoke after a replay and, five days before the FA Cup Final, clinched the League title by winning 1-0 at Tottenham of all places. Then, in the Final, we came from behind to defeat Liverpool 2-1 in extra time.

It was getting harder all the time. We had to play 64 matches in all that season — 51 in pursuit of the double, eight in the Fairs Cup, which we had won the year previously, and five in the League Cup.

FUNSPOT

TODAY'S CLUBS — LONG AGO

Many League clubs were formerly known by different names. Who would you have been watching if you had seen the following matches?

1. St Jude's v Pine Villa
2. Argyle Athletic v Newton Heath
3. Black Arabs v Bristol South End
4. Small Heath Alliance v Singers
5. New Brompton v Ardwick
6. Heaton Norrish Rovers v Abbey United

Answers on page 77

In 1970-1 Arsenal did the double in the most memorable season of my football life.

This was our record:

ARSENAL 1970-1

	P	W	D	L	F	A	Pts
Championship	42	29	7	6	71	29	65
FA Cup	9	6	3	0	16	7	—
	51	35	10	6	87	36	—

In 1972 Leeds United missed the double by the narrowest of margins, losing their last League game at Wolves, two days after beating Arsenal in the FA Cup Final.

Five years later, in 1976-7, came Liverpool's bid for the treble. On FA Cup semi-final day they were on top of the First Division, level on points with Manchester City and with a game in hand. Three days before the semi-final they beat Zurich to reach the European Cup Final.

A 3-0 replay win (after a 2-2 draw) against Everton took Liverpool to Wembley but there they lost the FA Cup Final 2-1 to Manchester United. With the Championship won, they went to Rome a few days later and beat Borussia Munchengladbach 3-1 to complete the different double of League Championship and European Cup.

When Ipswich played Manchester City at Villa Park in last season's FA Cup semi-final, they were three points behind Aston Villa with a game in hand and three days after the semi-final were due back at Villa Park for a rearranged League match. Two victories would have made them certainties for the double but, after missing several good chances early in the Cup game, they lost 1-0 to City in extra-time . . . and the dream was gone.

Ipswich showed remarkable powers of recovery by winning that League match at Villa Park 2-1 to hoist themselves back into the title race.

But the following Saturday, it all blew up in their faces. They lost 2-0 at home to Arsenal — and if any result cost the East Anglian club the title it was that one. Villa were never headed.

Ipswich went on toiling and when they finished as UEFA Cup winners they had played 66 matches against Villa's 46. Ironically, the team who eased Villa's fixture

Ipswich captain Mick Mills holds aloft the UEFA Cup.

problems by dumping them out of the FA Cup in the third round was . . . Ipswich, 1-0 winners at Portman Road.

Within two matches, 66 (including five in the League Cup) to 64, there is a great similarity between Ipswich and Arsenal's double-winning team. We, too, were hard pressed in Europe but I thought that last season Ipswich had every ingredient to achieve the double.

Bertie Mee, Arsenal's manager in the 'double year', skipper Frank McLintock and I happened to meet just before the FA Cup semi-final and we agreed that there was no way they could lose it.

They had class players, excellent leadership from manager Bobby Robson and captain Mick Mills and appeared to have the ability to surmount injuries. Kevin Beattie was then fit, Steve McCall was the unsung hero who had enabled George Burley's absence through injury to be carried and Kevin O'Callaghan was an able replacement for any of the strikers.

Right-back Burley, out for the season, was joined by Beattie, who broke his arm in the semi-final against Manchester City, and former first-team central defender Allan Hunter, whose cartilage went.

But Arsenal's double team had their problems, too Peter Simpson, our central defender, was out for a long spell with a knee injury and Charlie George broke a bone in a leg and missed most of the first half of the season.

Arsenal's double team had their luck in the Cup Final when three Liverpool defenders made a terrible botch-up and allowed Eddie Kelly and George Graham, between them, to score the winner.

Without that sort of luck, and Ipswich didn't have it, yes . . the double DOES get harder all the time.

DID YOU KNOW?

Which Football League player scored all his team's First Division goals in one season — and none of them counted? Sounds like a trick question . . . and Tommy Lawton, England centre-forward of his time, is the answer.

Season 1939-40 started on 26 August, and after three games Everton, the reigning League Champions, had three points and five goals — all of them scored by Lawton. Then, on 3 September, war broke out. That Football League programme was abandoned and the competition was not resumed until season 1946-7.

PERSONAL CHOICE

by Bob Wilson

● **My team as a boy:**
Manchester United — the Busby Babes (Duncan Edwards, Tommy Taylor, Roger Byrne etc). In 1957, I was with the club on schoolboy forms, having played for England Schoolboys with Nobby Stiles.

● **Career background:**
Born Chesterfield 1941; Chesterfield Grammar School; Loughborough College 1960-3; Arsenal 1964-74; Scotland 1971-2.

● **My first football assignment for BBC tv:**
In 1969. I was out of action with Arsenal, having broken an arm against Burnley, and was asked to put together a major goalkeeping item for *Sportsnight.* In my first 'live' studio piece, also about goalkeepers, I said 'tremendous' no fewer than 13 times. My wife counted!

● **Other sports I have commentated on:**
A shooting international at Bisley and international fencing.

● **Most memorable matches I have covered:**
Hamburg v Real Madrid (European Cup semi-final 1980). Hamburg, two down on the first leg, won the return — the game I was covering — 5-1, inspired by Kevin Keegan; the other was the 1979 FA Cup Final, Arsenal v Manchester United — memorable to me for its last six minutes. I wonder why!

● **My kind of football reading:**
Anything about football, except those former/current player 'revelation' series or stories, which infuriate me. They are totally destructive to the good of the game and generally cheap and ugly. In short, a disgrace.

● **Change in the game I would like to see:**
An improvement in the attitude of players, managers and coaches to defensive play. We should cater for the day and age in which we live and provide greater comfort and entertainment value.

● **Most exciting player in Britain today:**
I don't like giving one, especially when men like Keegan and Dalglish are such a pleasure to watch. However, Glenn Hoddle, of Spurs, has a touch of genius . . . yes, I'll settle for him among the younger players.

● **The match I wish I could have covered:**
England 3, Hungary 6 at Wembley on 25 November 1953. The Magyars provided some brilliant moments and their performance taught me, as an aspiring young footballer, that no-one can ever rest on his laurels.

● **Among my souvenirs:**
Personally signed copy of Pele's autobiography. Having interviewed him, I was given the book and, on leaving the hotel room, I was stopped by an elderly lady cleaner. She obviously knew the Brazilian ace was staying at the hotel but had no idea what he looked like . . . as I gathered when she said to me: 'Excuse me. Are you Pele!!!'

● **My biggest gaff on the air:**
November 1977 — on my match report (Chelsea 1, Nottingham Forest 0) for *Grandstand,* I said: 'I think Forest's bubble will burst.' They finished the season as champions. Sorry, Brian!

● **Match moment I'll never forget:**
The 1956 FA Cup Final. Manchester City goalkeeper Bert Trautmann, my idol, diving at the feet of Birmingham's Peter Murphy, breaking his neck and playing on to victory.

● **Managers I admire most:**
Pre-war . . . Herbert Chapman, who achieved two League Championship hat-tricks, with Huddersfield Town and Arsenal. Unbelievable! Post-war . . . Sir Matt Busby. To win with style as he did after the Munich air disaster belongs among the great achievements in British football.

● **Personality of the past I would like to have interviewed:**
Bert Trautmann who, from being a German prisoner-of-war, earned total acceptance by British fans as Manchester City's goalkeeper and Footballer of the Year. It was a great thrill to meet him at Wembley last Cup Final day.

● **The man I would like to see manage England when Ron Greenwood retires:**
Bobby Robson, of Ipswich, with Arsenal's Don Howe as his assistant. They would be a perfect combination, as two of the best coaches and deepest thinkers in England.

● **The man I think will get the job when Ron Greenwood retires:**
Bobby Robson.

● **1982 World Cup winners:**
I can't decide between West Germany, the best prepared and most powerful European team, and Brazil, the world's most naturally talented footballers, who will feel completely at home in the heat of Spain.

PERSONAL CHOICE

HALL OF FAME · HALL OF FAME · HALL OF FAME · HALL OF FAME · HALL OF FAME

DEREK HALES struck his most prolific scoring form in 1980-1, totalling 17 goals in Charlton's Third Division promotion success. It was his third season back with Charlton after spells with Derby and West Ham. In his first spell with Charlton, he scored 73 goals, having joined them from Luton in October 1973 (£10,000). He moved to Derby in December 1976 (£280,000) and returned to London with West Ham in September 1977 (£110,000). Then, in July 1978, aged 26, he rejoined Charlton at £75,000.

HALL OF FAME · HALL OF FAME · HALL OF FAME · HALL OF FAME

HALL OF FAME · HALL OF FAME · HALL OF FAME · HALL OF FAME · HALL OF FAME

HALL OF FAME · HALL OF FAME · HALL OF FAME · HALL OF FAME · HALL OF FAME · HALL OF FAME ·

JOHN WARK, of Ipswich Town, was Britain's top marksman last season with 35 goals — more than double his total in 1979-80. His enormous contribution to Ipswich's bid for triple honours earned him, at 23, the PFA 'Player of the Year' Award. Two factors contributed to his prodigious scoring rate: the knack of advancing from midfield into the right place at the right time and an almost unerring right-foot accuracy from the penalty-spot. He joined Ipswich from Drumchapel Amateurs, Glasgow, in 1973. Scottish International.

HALL OF FAME · HALL OF FAME · HALL OF FAME · HALL OF FAME ·

CRAIG JOHNSTON, Liverpool's 21-year-old midfield star, was born in South Africa (Johannesburg) and reared in Australia (New South Wales). Last March Middlesbrough accepted an offer of £500,000 from Anfield for the England Under 21 mid-field attacker, and, although it was at first agreed that he should see out his contract with Boro', he in fact signed for Liverpool on 3 April. Craig, discovered at 14 when Boro' toured Australia, had set his heart on a career in England after watching *Match of the Day* 12,000 miles away.

HALL OF FAME · HALL OF FAME · HALL OF FAME · HALL OF FAME

PETER McCLOY, of Rangers — Peter the Giant, all 6ft 4in and nearly 15st of him — has been at Ibrox since March 1970, when he joined Rangers from Kilmarnock. He won his first full cap for Scotland against Wales in May 1973 and played in three other internationals at the end of that season. His sound, consistent and often brilliant form between the posts has helped Rangers to win three Championships, three League Cups and the Scottish FA Cup four times.

Do you share your

JANUARY

1	Tony Currie
2	
3	
4	Mick Mills
5	David Fairclough
6	
7	
8	
9	
10	Steve Moran
11	Bryan Robson (WBA)
12	
13	
14	
15	
16	Dixie McNeil
17	
18	
19	
20	
21	Phil Thompson
22	
23	Frans Thijssen
24	
25	Phil Boyer
26	Jim Platt
27	
28	Kenny Swain
29	
30	Mark Proctor
31	

FEBRUARY

1	Franco Causio
2	
3	
4	
5	
6	Brendon Batson
7	Sammy Lee
8	Tommy Langley
9	Cyrille Regis
10	Jimmy Rimmer
11	
12	
13	Liam Brady
14	Kevin Keegan (Southampton)
15	
16	
17	
18	
19	Justin Fashanu
20	Phil Neal
21	
22	
23	
24	
25	Ally Dawson
26	
27	
28	Dino Zoff

MARCH

1	
2	
3	
4	Kenny Dalglish
5	Petar Borota
6	Martin Buchan
7	
8	Laurie Cunningham (Real Madrid)
9	John Wile
10	Garth Crooks
11	
12	
13	
14	
15	
16	
17	Pat Rice
18	David Moss
19	
20	
21	
22	
23	Robbie James
24	Rudi Krol
25	
26	
27	
28	
29	Rainer Bonhof
30	
31	

APRIL

1	Dai Davies
2	
3	
4	
5	Dennis Mortimer
6	
7	
8	Joe Royle
9	
10	
11	
12	
13	
14	Milija Aleksic
15	
16	
17	
18	
19	Trevor Francis (Nott'm Forest)
20	
21	
22	
23	
24	
25	
26	
27	
28	Paul Bradshaw
29	
30	Gerry Daly

MAY

1	Danny McGrain
2	David O'Leary
3	
4	Trevor Whymark
5	
6	Graeme Souness (Liverpool)
7	Micky Droy
8	Dave Provan
9	
10	
11	
12	
13	
14	
15	
16	
17	
18	Jimmy Case
19	
20	Clive Allen
21	
22	Paul Mariner
23	Ian Wallace
24	
25	
26	
27	
28	
29	
30	
31	

JUNE

1	
2	Mark Lawrenson
3	George Burley
4	
5	
6	Gary Rowell
7	Lou Macari
8	
9	
10	Peter Barnes
11	
12	Pat Jennings
13	Alan Hansen
14	
15	Alan Brazil
16	
17	
18	
19	
20	
21	
22	Kevin Bond
23	
24	
25	Clive Walker
26	Gordon McQueen (Man United)
27	
28	
29	
30	

birthday with a star?

JULY

1	Alan Sunderland
2	
3	
4	
5	
6	
7	Gary Owen
8	Steve Hunt
9	Steve Coppell
10	Frank Stapleton
11	
12	
13	
14	Arthur Albiston
15	Mario Kempes
16	John Hollins
17	
18	
19	
20	
21	Brian Talbot
22	
23	
24	
25	
26	
27	
28	Ray Kennedy (Liverpool)
29	Viv Anderson
30	
31	

AUGUST

1	
2	Peter Eastoe
3	Osvaldo Ardiles (Tottenham)
4	John Wark
5	Ray Clemence
6	
7	
8	Phil Parkes
9	Gary Bailey
10	
11	
12	
13	Peter Wells
14	
15	
16	
17	
18	
19	
20	
21	
22	
23	
24	
25	
26	Tony Morley
27	
28	Emlyn Hughes
29	
30	Peter Wythe
31	Alan Kennedy

SEPTEMBER

1	
2	
3	
4	
5	
6	
7	Ray Stewart
8	
9	
10	
11	
12	
13	
14	Ray Wilkins
15	
16	
17	Billy Bonds
18	Peter Shilton (Nott'm Forest)
19	
20	Frank Lampard
21	
22	Tommy Hutchison
23	Kenny Burns
24	
25	
26	Kenny Sansom
27	Steve Archibald
28	Kevin Arnott
29	Karl-Heinz Rummenigge
30	

OCTOBER

1	
2	Trevor Brooking (West Ham)
3	
4	
5	Dave Watson
6	Tommy Caton
7	
8	
9	
10	Vince Hilaire
11	
12	Allan Evans
13	
14	
15	
16	Steve Buckley
17	
18	
19	
20	Romeo Benetti
21	
22	
23	David Johnson
24	Asa Hartford
25	
26	Arthur Graham
27	Glenn Hoddle
28	Gordon Cowans
29	
30	Diego Maradona
31	Steve Wicks

NOVEMBER

1	
2	Kenny Hector
3	
4	
5	
6	
7	
8	Alan Curbishley
9	Tommy Booth
10	
11	
12	Kevin Ratcliffe
13	
14	Remi Moses
15	Ulrich Steilike
16	Arni Haan
17	
18	Joe Corrigan
19	
20	
21	
22	
23	
24	
25	Willie Young
26	Peter McCloy
27	
28	Mike Channon
29	
30	Andy Gray (Wolves)

DECEMBER

1	
2	
3	
4	
5	
6	Stan Cumming
7	
8	Terry McDermott (Liverpool)
9	
10	
11	John Lukic
12	
13	
14	
15	Joe Jordan
16	Tommy Burns
17	
18	
19	
20	Irving Nattras
21	Paul Cooper
22	Bernd Schuster
23	
24	
25	
26	David Armstrong
27	Roberto Bettega
28	Jimmy Nicholl
29	
30	Charlie Nicholas
31	

GLENN HODDLE

–the name that spells hope for England's future

by Barry Davies

SIX DAYS early last May said a great deal about English football. On the Saturday Manchester City, by stifling the natural creative instincts of key players of the Spurs team, very nearly left Wembley with the FA Cup. The following Tuesday Brazil won there for the first time, scoring the one goal during a dazzling 20 minutes which had England chasing shadows. The watching Spurs team gained a rather different impression of the game from the media, which emphasised how well the home team recovered. And two days later their own South Americans, the Argentines Ardiles and Villa, enjoyed to the full the delayed celebration of victory in the 100th Final.

Two of the goals that night, Mackenzie's for City and Villa's remarkable winner for Spurs, truly belonged with the festive atmosphere which the Brazilians had created and which carried over to a match of far greater competition. And the architect of Tottenham's success, for all the fact that he would not have looked out of place in either, came from neither Cordoba nor the Copacabana.

As Ron Greenwood put it a week later, musing with affection over the open style of Brazil's football, which during their three-match European tour established them as favourites to win the World Cup in Spain: 'In England we play football which is closed down before we start.' But at Wembley, on 14 May, Glenn Hoddle, in a balanced side, beat the system.

Hoddle's shot is deflected into the net . . . and the 100th FA Cup Final goes to a replay.

With the justifiable pride of a father, Derek Hoddle says that Wembley is tailor-made for his son. What the son has to prove is that he is tailor-made for the urgent needs of England. Comment that 'there is no way I will have done that until I have won 30 or 40 caps', may surprise critics of his application and give hope to those who would like to see an undoubted talent take more matches by the scruff of the neck.

'Two years ago, it didn't matter what anyone said — I knew that I just didn't have the strength to do it. But I now feel as fit in the last ten minutes as I do in the first ten. I know that people would like to see me stamp my authority on more games and hopefully I shall be able to do it one day for England,' said Hoddle.

Glenn is one of those lucky people who have no need to understand the saying, 'Relations are forced upon us, thank God we can choose our friends'. He is blessed with a father who knew how to treat a son who had more talent than he himself had for the game he loves; a mother, who, apart from living up to the true meaning of that word, is a genuine football enthusiast; a young uncle who, by his own admittance, showed Glenn what can happen if a player doesn't apply himself; and a brother, ten years his junior, who, by following in his footsteps, affords the opportunity to set an example.

The family in every sense is big with the Hoddles. There were 36 of them at Wembley last Cup Final day and almost as many when he played his first full match for Spurs at Stoke on 21 February, 1976. Says Glenn: 'The atmosphere really bubbled at home that evening. I remember they put banners up on the door and next day we bought every paper which covered the match.' They recorded the fact that a fine performance had been capped with a brilliant winning goal, hit from 25 yards.

To say that it came as no surprise to Derek Hoddle or even, perhaps, to his son is not to suggest arrogance in either but simply a belief in both. Dad will tell you that the first time he rolled a coloured ball to his toddler, Glenn kicked it back. 'A little later,' Glenn recalls, 'he'd be over in the park with me playing for hours at a time to the point where he'd have to leave me sitting under a tree, crying and asking for just one more shot.

'But with all the help and advice he's given me over the years — and he's still a very honest critic — the best thing about Dad was

DID YOU KNOW?

The cockerel, perched with lofty grace on top of the Tottenham stand, has been Spurs' emblem since 1909 and over the years has looked down on some of football's finest talents and greatest triumphs. The bird, made of copper, was installed when that stand was erected (opposite the £3 million stand that opened this season). The measurements are: height 5ft; 3ft 6in from beak to tail; 15in thick and mounted on a copper ball that is 31in in diameter. The cost was £35.

What's inside the ball? Souvenir documents of Tottenham's admission to the First Division in 1909 and some coins of that period.

that he knew when to leave me alone, when to keep in the background. He never pushed too hard or tried to tell the coaches they were wrong. And he's always told me "listen to what people say to you but in the end do what you believe is right".'

Son describes father as 'very skilful and very good in the air, which is not one of my strengths'. Derek played for a number of top amateur clubs like Harlow, Ware and Windsor & Eton. His brother was good enough to have made it as a goalkeeper at Spurs but for a 'Jack the lad' attitude which he was later able to turn to Glenn's advantage after years of 'being put between the trees' on some of those afternoons in the park.

Doing things with the ball were what those hours were about and what now separates Glenn Hoddle from his contemporaries. 'I remember one afternoon when Dad and Dave wanted to time me to see how long I could keep the ball in the air. In the end they had to go indoors.'

'On the ball he's magic,' says his father. 'At times he does things which make my eyes pop out of my head. He's never going to be a great tackler, but it is about balance — you've got to find other people who can do that.' Like, for example, Steve Perryman, another important influence on Glenn's career. 'I think I have improved the defensive side of my game from 25 per cent to 70 per cent in the last couple of years and I owe a lot to Steve. He tells me that if I can make them knock balls square or back I've done my job. Defence is not just about crunching tackles, though I must say I enjoyed those I made in the Cup Final replay. But my game is about going forward; that's what makes me happy and I think 70-30 is the right balance.'

Glenn's respect for Spurs' captain is such that he believes he should have won many caps for England — and if Alf Ramsey had stayed he would have!

His own chance, after being a member of the winning England Youth side of 1975 and rather too many 'trials' with the Under 21s, came in November 1979 against Bulgaria at Wembley.

'As it was my first time in the senior squad, I really didn't expect to play. I thought I was there for the experience.' Instead the experience was given to those who were watching, as Glenn hit one of those spectacular goals which have become something of a trademark.

That he has had a struggle to command a regular England place at a time when there is a desperate need for players of true

Glenn Hoddle in action . . . his game is about balance and 'going forward — that's what makes me happy'

international quality is a disappointment, not least to Hoddle himself. But he is very much more aware of the truth of the remark made by his club manager, Keith Burkinshaw, that skilful players cannot expect others to let them play and more conscious of his team role than outsiders might believe.

'I know I could go out there and not give the ball away. But I'd cut my ability in half, so I look for the balls which are more difficult. And the more progressive balls you play, the greater is the chance that some will get cut out. But those that get through are the ones

that win matches. I think I play more of them now at the right time — that's experience.'

Off the field, though, experience, as his five best friends, mates from school, will tell you, hasn't changed him. He's still very much the same lad who, when people told him from a very early age what a good player he was, 'had a funny feeling they were making it all up. I never let myself believe it. If I had, I suppose it might have gone to my head.

'Being a family person has been very important, as was the fact that I joined the club down the road [an association that began when Glenn was 11]. I've seen a lot of players who have moved to other areas at the beginning of their careers go off the rails, and I suppose it could have happened to me.'

FUNSPOT

MOORE THE MERRIER

The answer to each of the following five questions is a year. Add all the numbers to find out how many caps Bobby Moore won for England.

In which year did . . .

1. West Ham play in Wembley's first Cup Final?
2. Bobby Moore play his first League game for West Ham?
3. Bobby Moore play his last for West Ham?
4. West Ham pay the record goalkeeper fee for Phil Parkes?
5. West Ham reach the European Cup-Winners' Cup Final for the second time?

Answers on page 77

Of all the players that night at Wembley last May, Hoddle was the one most emotionally affected by the Cup victory . . . which surprised him rather more than it did his mother. And during the summer he had to balance the joy of that success and the possibility of more with Spurs against the desire to test his talents abroad.

There were many other factors: his family, the wishes of his wife, Anne, his headmaster's daughter whom he first took out at 14 (who, incidentally, speaks both French and German) and the possibility of starting a further line of Hoddles. Then there were the arguments of financial security and what might be lost or gained in World Cup terms.

In the end, the decision was down to him: just as, given the good sense of those who select, how well he uses his gifts is down to him — what he does with a life whose course was decided from the moment his mother carried her baby son to watch his father play football.

In case he should ever forget his own definition of a world-class player, let it be here in black and white for him to refer to: 'A world-class player is one you could put in any side, in any country, playing any system and he could adapt.'

Of those to whom much is given, much is required.

PERSONAL CHOICE

by Barry Davies

My team as a boy:

As bias is the most common criticism of a commentator, I have never revealed which team I supported as a boy. For the same reason, I'll leave out my birthplace, too.

Career background:

I was educated at Cranbrook School, Kent (as were Peter West and Brian Moore) and London University. I did my first broadcast for BFN Cologne (it is now called British Forces Broadcasting Services and I still often introduce their main sports programme, *London Sportsdesk*). I worked unofficially for BBC Radio's *Sports Report* for ten months (I was only ever contracted for Saturdays — pay £6). I joined *The Times,* initially as a sub-editor and later I reported for them. I took leave to work for ITV at the 1966 World Cup Finals. In September of that year I joined ABC Television as commentator on their *World of Soccer* programme. I came to the BBC in July 1969 — transfer fee undisclosed.

My first football assignment for BBCtv:

I introduced Wales v Rest of UK, a special match on 28 July, 1969 to mark the Investiture of the Prince of Wales. My first commentary was on 9 August that year. I began the day in Leeds, expecting to cover their match against Spurs. But David Coleman was taken ill and I was rushed by car to London, commentated on Crystal Palace v Manchester United (2-2) in the afternoon and introduced the first new-style *Match of the Day* in the evening.

Club ground with the best facilities for TV coverage:

I rate Anfield and Old Trafford as joint first choice.

Other sports I've commentated on:

The major ones in TV coverage terms are athletics and badminton. But, including Olympic and Commonwealth Games, I have also covered hockey, handball, volleyball, cycling, cyclocross, and water-skiing.

Most memorable match I have covered:

The 1977 European Cup Final in Rome between Liverpool and Borussia Munchengladbach. It was a marvellous, fluctuating match with the best possible finish for the English Champions. After their FA Cup Final defeat by Manchester United four days earlier, it was a very emotional occasion. At the end, I felt totally drained.
Next best: Argentina v France — the 'quality' match of the last World Cup.

The match I wish I could have covered:

The 1960 European Cup Final between Real Madrid and Eintracht Frankfurt (7-3) because of the sheer quality of the football.

Changes in the game I would like to see:

That three points for a win was needed was an indictment of attitudes. Sport is about winning, not about not losing. One change I have long advocated is being applied by the better referees, who give themselves time to see if an advantage can be gained by the side against whom an infringement has been committed.

Among my souvenirs:

A signed programme from my first televised match, Chelsea v AC Milan, on 16 February, 1966. It reads: 'Barry, here's to the first of many' and is signed 'Jimmy Greaves'.

My biggest broadcasting gaff:

Giving a goal to Gerry Gow which was scored for Bristol City by Geoff Merrick. It was a total misidentification which I still can't explain. I'll always remember Geoff's comment: 'I wouldn't mind — but I don't score many'.

Moment of magic I'll never forget:

Pele's dummy on Mazurkievicz, the Uruguayan goalkeeper, in the 1970 World Cup semi-final. In the same match he volleyed back the 'keeper's misdirected goal-kick from 35 yards. Incredible genius.

I'd give him a medal:

Not 'him' but 'her'. My wife — for understanding what the work of a sports commentator involves. And, in pure TV terms, for being my most informative critic.

The man I would like to see manage England when Ron Greenwood retires:

Jack Charlton because he has the knowledge and would be pragmatic in his approach. And because he would, I think, be able to live with the inevitable criticism.

The man I think will get the job when Ron Greenwood retires:

Bobby Robson.

1982 World Cup winners:

The West Germans will take a deal of beating.

PERSONAL CHOICE

My verdict on the transfer market

by Lawrie McMenemy

talking to Brian Gearing

BY THE TIME the curtain dropped on Britain's 1980-81 soccer season, eight British footballers had been transferred for one million pounds or more with young Clive Allen, who ended up at Crystal Palace, involved in two million-plus deals.

For a few short months the transfer market went stark, raving mad. In fact, I'd say that only the first million-pound man, Trevor Francis, who went from Birmingham to Nottingham Forest for £1,180,000 in February 1979, was worth the money he cost. Trevor has the kind of rare talent that means that any manager would splash whatever money he's got available to acquire his services.

But that spell of big-spending was an inflationary burst that need not, and should not, have happened. It's over now, thank goodness — halted by the harsh facts of Britain's present-day economic life. Many clubs are struggling financially as attendance figures continue to fall and there just isn't the money about to meet the cost of soaring fees.

The transfer market, the buying and selling of players, is a necessary part of the professional game. Amateurs and professionals play football to the same rules, but the difference is that the professional game is a business. As with any business, money is involved.

Professional clubs obtain their money from their 'gates' — which, as I say, are not the source of revenue they once were — and, increasingly, through commercial activities such as lotteries and club shops. They spend their money on players' wages and bonuses, on travel, equipment and ground maintenance. And they spend it on strengthening their team by buying players. They open their purse, see what they've got to spend — and go shopping.

You might buy an established star in his prime, a ready-made, tried and tested player; that's the safest way to proceed but also, of course, the most costly. You might buy a promising youngster and hope that he's got the character to go on developing his obvious natural talent. Or you might buy a senior player who's past his prime but still has a valuable contribution to make.

The latter course is one that I have followed at Southampton. In fact, many people have told me that I buy only 'old men'. The truth is that Southampton haven't the money to be able to buy star players in their mid-twenties.

Trevor Francis was the first British footballer to cost a million; Clive Allen (pictured left) got in on the act twice.

DID YOU KNOW?

The official attendance for the first FA Cup final played at Wembley — on 28 April 1923, when Bolton Wanderers beat West Ham United 2-0 — broke all records. The FA official report stated: 'Because of the crowd breaking in, an accurate attendance return could not be made. The official return of the British Empire Exhibition authorities was that 90,520 people passed through the turnstiles and 35,527 ticket-holders were also admitted.

'That would give an attendance of 126,047 but there were probably 150,000 spectators present. The start of the match was delayed 40 minutes, owing to the crowd having invaded the playing pitch.

'According to statistics supplied by the railway companies, 241,000 passengers booked to the ground from London stations. The gross gate was £27,776. The two clubs and the FA each received £6365 1s 8d as their share of the receipts and the FA refunded £4000 from their portion to ticket-holders unable to get to their seats.'

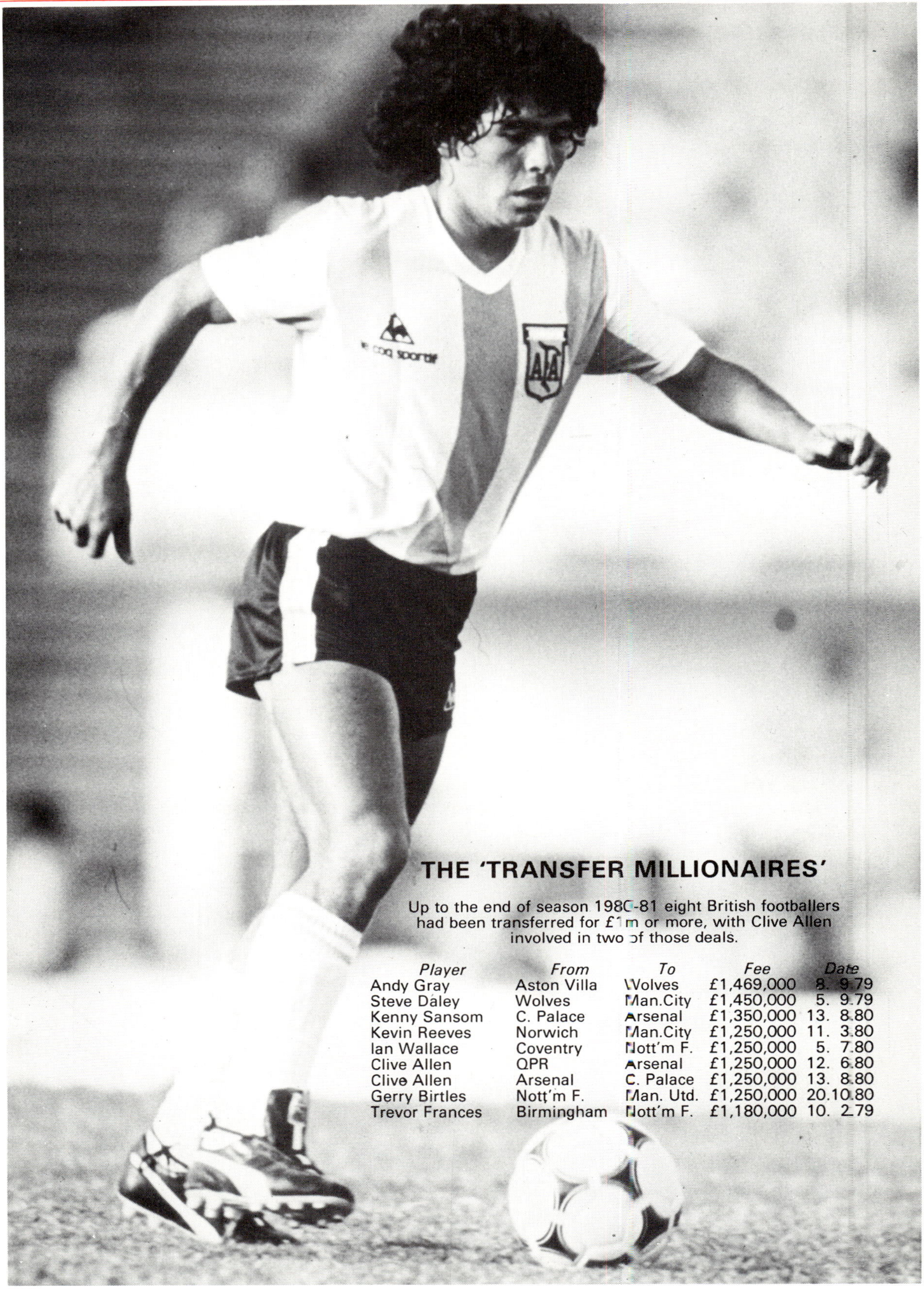

THE 'TRANSFER MILLIONAIRES'

Up to the end of season 1980-81 eight British footballers had been transferred for £1m or more, with Clive Allen involved in two of those deals.

Player	*From*	*To*	*Fee*	*Date*
Andy Gray	Aston Villa	Wolves	£1,469,000	8. 9.79
Steve Daley	Wolves	Man.City	£1,450,000	5. 9.79
Kenny Sansom	C. Palace	Arsenal	£1,350,000	13. 8.80
Kevin Reeves	Norwich	Man.City	£1,250,000	11. 3.80
Ian Wallace	Coventry	Nott'm F.	£1,250,000	5. 7.80
Clive Allen	QPR	Arsenal	£1,250,000	12. 6.80
Clive Allen	Arsenal	C. Palace	£1,250,000	13. 8.80
Gerry Birtles	Nott'm F.	Man. Utd.	£1,250,000	20.10.80
Trevor Frances	Birmingham	Nott'm F.	£1,180,000	10. 2.79

Only Kevin Keegan at £400,000 and Charlie George at £312,000 cost me more than £200,000.

As I told you in *Match of the Day* annual last year, Southampton's scouting network and youth policy — which I believe are as good as any in the country — enable us to produce many fine young players. Some of these come through to the first team and there, together with the experienced senior players I've bought, form a squad which has enabled Southampton to climb steadily up the First Division table in recent seasons. In three years we've progressed from 14th place to the top six.

In view of some of the cracks you may hear about Lawrie McMenemy's 'elderly' team, let me put the record straight. More than half my first team squad are young players, most of them — like Graham Baker, Steve Williams, Nick Holmes, Steve Moran and Reuben Agboola — all home-produced. Peter Wells is a youngster I bought — but he cost me only £8000.

We call our youth policy at Southampton the Conveyor Belt and some of the youngsters who come off that conveyor belt may not be sufficiently talented to win a regular place in the First Division. But often they are still good, competent professionals and able to do a valuable job for clubs in lower divisions. It is by the selling of players like these that we are able to fund our youth policy and help to raise the cash with which to buy senior players like Keegan, Watson, George, Channon and Ball.

So you can see that buying and selling goes on all the time. At Southampton over the last three years I've worked on an average net outlay of £400,000. When I tell you that the average transfer in the First Division is still around the £500,000 mark you'll see that the pace is still too hot for me.

Yet clubs like Southampton — Ipswich are another example — must compete with the big city clubs like Arsenal, Liverpool and Manchester United. We can do it only if our clubs are well run and if, when we go shopping, we proceed as carefully as a housewife watching her every penny. The truth is that if I'd gone after some of my 'old men' earlier I could not have afforded them.

Britain's economic plight apart, there are other factors at work trying to establish sanity in the transfer market. The Association of Secretaries and Managers have the Football League's support in seeking to curtail 'never-never' transfers. This is the system whereby clubs pay for a player in instalments; I've known cases where players have moved on before their previous fees have been paid up!

Then again, the players themselves, through the Professional Footballers' Association, have called for transfer fees to be limited to ten times a player's annual wage — a system which is applied in some European countries.

But if you believe that our transfer market has its madder moments, let me tell you about a situation which developed this year in Argentina. At the centre of it was the young player who is probably the hottest property in world football — Diego Maradona. Boca Juniors wanted to buy him from Argentino Juniors. The asking price was, wait for it — three million pounds. Boca Juniors agreed and then found they couldn't raise the money. So, in the end, Maradona went to them on loan for the season — for a fee of one-and-a-half million pounds.

I think that story should be a warning to all of us involved in the transfer market. We need it, yes — but, for the good of our game, commonsense must always prevail.

Left: Argentina's Diego Maradona — he's probably the hottest property in world football and was at the centre of one of the silliest transfer situations of them all!

FUNSPOT

SPOT THE TEAMS

Hidden in our secret box are the nicknames of 11 League clubs. They can be found horizontally, vertically, backwards or forwards.

S	R	E	N	N	U	G	O	P	G
B	L	U	E	B	I	R	D	S	R
E	S	L	A	E	S	J	L	E	O
E	W	N	S	E	L	A	D	O	B
S	K	B	L	R	T	D	O	O	I
H	G	G	I	I	E	O	Z	P	N
Y	A	T	C	V	E	M	M	P	S
E	L	S	I	B	T	A	M	F	S
O	J	L	I	S	T	N	I	A	S
L	S	E	I	P	G	A	M	W	H

Answers on page 77

CHARLIE NICHOLAS, of Celtic, enjoyed a truly triumphant first season. This 19-year-old striker scored some crackers in a total of 25 goals in 1980-1 and finished it with Scottish League Championship honours. What's more, his meteoric rise brought him caps at Youth and Under-21 levels. As he maintained a flow of goals for Celtic he was talked of, potentially as a Scotland goalscoring discovery in the class of Denis Law and Kenny Dalglish. He comes from Glasgow and began with Celtic Boys.

JEREMY CHARLES, of Swansea City, has the pedigree to become a world-class player — for he is the son of Mel Charles and nephew of John Charles, both great Welsh Internationals. Jeremy has played in defence, midfield and attack with equal effect. He made his first-team debut at 16 and became captain of Swansea at 21. His first senior game for Wales was in November 1980 and he finished the season with four caps, having also helped Swansea all the way from Fourth Division to First in four seasons.

GARRY THOMPSON, of Coventry City, a 21-year-old, Birmingham-born striker, made headlines with two goals when Coventry beat West Ham 3-2 in the League Cup semi-final first leg last season. He also scored an own-goal that night — and claimed the match-ball for his 'hat-trick'! The former England Youth cap, whose early progress was checked when he broke a leg in training, is one of the Sky Blues' young stars of quality, and he played in the last three Under-21 Internationals of season 1980-1

PETER EASTOE, of Everton, is the striker who found that Merseyside suited him best of all after moving to Goodison Park from QPR in March 1979 — valued at £280,000 in an exchange involving Mick Walsh. He began his career with Wolves, then joined Swindon in March 1974 (£80,000) and QPR in March 1976 (£90,000), signed by Dave Sexton to boost a Championship challenge in which they finished runners-up to Liverpool. He was Everton's top scorer last season with 19 goals.

Sometimes we do the talking

by
Alan Parry

The Commentators line-up before the kick-off. That's me third from the left in the back row. On my right is Tony Gubba and in the centre of the front row is John Motson.

IF THE SCENE had been captured by the *Match of the Day* cameras, Jimmy Hill and Bob Wilson would have had a field day! The voices of John Motson, Tony Gubba and myself were being heard in millions of homes — but the audience could never have guessed what the owners of those voices were doing as the famous signature tune brought another

vith our feet!

show to a close.

The intrepid trio could be found stark naked, freezing cold, covered from head to toe with mud. They were standing, in semi-darkness, in an old wooden shed in the middle of a field, being drenched by buckets of icy water thrown at them by so-called colleagues!

Former rugby star Gareth Edwards (left) in a soccer role. He shakes hands with Commentators' skipper, Steve Hamer.

It may sound like a bizarre adventure from Monty Python . . . but it was, in fact, a typical day out for the enthusiasts who form The Commentators Eleven, Britain's only team of footballing commentators.

On the day in question, the team was in action in one of their less glamorous fixtures. A park pitch so muddy you could have grown rice on it; a dressing-room that would have been a condemned building even in a shanty-town . . . and, inevitably, no sign of a shower or hot bath (hence those buckets of cold water!).

But in the ten years since they were formed, the Commentators XI has appeared on top grounds all over the country and raised many thousands of pounds for charity. They've turned out at Anfield, The Hawthorns and Ashton Gate — but also paraded their skills at more unlikely venues to help out a local scout group or village school.

They've even been into Europe! In 1977, and again in 1979, the Commentators XI packed their boots and went on tour, playing matches on the Spanish mainland and on the island of Majorca. And the summer of 1981 saw the most ambitious trip yet — a two-week stay in Florida with matches on the ground of Tampa Bay Rowdies, the American club managed by an Englishman, Gordon Jago.

Over the years, some of the best-known

names in football have "guested" for the Commentators XI. Jimmy Greaves, Ron Atkinson, Terry Neill, Keith Burkinshaw, Frank McLintock, Don Howe, Peter Mellor and Teddy Maybank are just some that I can recall. And the opposition has included celebrity teams from the world of show-business, tennis and horse-racing.

So, why do we do it? When so much of our lives is spent reporting football for the BBC, why do we give up our free time actually to play the game?

Well, for a start we all enjoy it, but I think John Motson, a founder member of the team, speaks for us all when he says that playing football — no matter what the standard might be — makes you become a better commentator.

Says John: 'Playing, even at our level, makes you realise how little time and space you get on a football field. From the commentary position — and, of course, on the television screen — the pitch can look massive and the game can look easy.

'But from my own playing experience on Sunday afternoons I've learned to appreciate just how difficult the game can be. I always think twice before criticising a player for a mistake . . . it's easy to be flippant in commentary when you don't appreciate how hard it is for the players.'

When John left school and started his first job as a reporter on a weekly newspaper in North London, he helped to form a journalists' football team known as the Roving Reporters. He is now club president.

And come the day he has to hang up his boots, John is keen to turn his hand to coaching, having gained his Football Association Preliminary Coaching Badge at Lilleshall in 1973.

I, too, have been on an FA coaching course, at Bisham Abbey, but my love for kicking a ball around began in a very different setting. I was born and bred in Liverpool and as a youngster spent every spare moment out in the street playing football.

We used to have games of about 25-a-side in a narrow, terraced street, playing with a tennis ball. The games would go on for hours and the only stoppages were for broken windows or the appearance of the local bobby!

Later, I played for my school team, the youth club side and a couple of pub teams, in that order! Playing in the Liverpool Sunday League was quite an experience. The matches weren't exactly gentle and I think that's where I acquired my well-known robust

Just look at the commitment from Tony Gubba and Co. We really give it our all! From the commentary position, the game can look easy. Our matches are a sure way of reminding us that it most certainly isn't . . .

style and fiery temperament!

Still, injuries apart, playing football has given me as much pleasure as commentating on the game. I have some great memories, like playing in a Liverpool jersey in front of 45,000 fans at Anfield. That was on the night of Tommy Smith's testimonial game in 1977. And during the European Championship in Italy in 1980, I played for a 'Rest of the World' press team against the Italian journalists — and the whole game was shown on Italian television!

I certainly agree with John Motson when he says that playing football makes you a better commentator. The same goes for any sport. When I became a regular commentator on athletics for BBC Radio I took up running for the first time since schooldays.

Wheezing around my local track in 5½ minutes for a mile made me appreciate just how good the likes of Seb Coe and Steve Ovett really are.

But back to the Commentators XI. One of the stars of the side over the years has been another *Match of the Day* celebrity, Bob Wilson.

But those who've seen us play will know that lurking inside that great goalkeeper for all those years was an aggressive striker just bursting to get out!

Persuading Bob to play in goal these days is one of the most difficult tasks in football. All he wants to do is pull on a number 9 jersey, get the ball at his feet and head for goal.

'Yes, I really enjoy the chance to play out of goal,' Bob told me. 'There've been some very enjoyable matches over the years. It can only be beneficial to the lads who didn't play League football to be involved in these charity games every week. I'm sure it gives them an appreciation of the players' problems.

'The standard doesn't really matter. What's important is that they're getting involved and finding out what it's like to have only a split second to control the ball.

'It's a pet theory of mine that all commentators — and football reporters — should take the FA's Preliminary Coaching Award and also sit an exam on the Laws of

FUNSPOT

WHOSE IS THE BADGE?

Whose club badges feature the following?

1. Sword
2. Horse
3. Fox
4. Stag
5. Robin
6. Three fishes and a boat
7. Owl
8. Windmill
9. Knight on horseback
10. Magpie

Answers on page 77

the Game, as referees do.

'Actually playing the game every week is a bonus — but obviously you can't go on playing forever.'

Well, I've told you that Bob Wilson is a bustling centre-forward, so what about the rest of the team? Yours truly fancies himself as a cross between the attacking Phil Neal and the tough-tackling Tommy Smith. My team-mates might say otherwise!

My full-back partner is Tony Gubba. He's brave and quick, but admits to being a little out of condition these days.

John Motson is our midfield dynamo. An accurate passer of the ball, he's one of the fittest members of the side.

Producer John Rowlinson is a tricky left-winger who has played in the second team for Fourth Division Crewe Alexandra, where his father has been club chairman for many years.

Steve Walford (no, not that one!) is a vital member of the *Match of the Day* backroom team — and of Commentators XI defence.

And now I must let you into a secret. Despite our intense rivalry on the screen, BBC and ITV do join forces every Sunday on the playing fields of England. Two key members of the Commentators side are Jim Rosenthal, of London Weekend, and Yorkshire TV's Martin Tyler. Ian St.John makes an occasional appearance, too.

The side is completed by pals of ours like Gordon Riddick, who played over 400 League games for Charlton, Luton and Gillingham; Robin Russell, one of the FA's top staff coaches; Keith East, another former League player who was a prolific goalscorer with a host of different clubs; Steve Hamer, former player-manager of the famous amateur side, Corinthian Casuals; plus schoolteacher Mick Dobner and solicitor Pete Walford.

Over the years, other *Match of the Day* commentators Barry Davies and Desmond Lynam and former editor Mike Murphy (now editor of *Grandstand*) have also turned out.

How long can we keep going? Well, when the matches are over and we all adjourn to the bar, the average age of the team is one of the most heated talking points. Suffice to say

Referee! John Motson makes an urgent appeal — it looks just like a scene from Match of the Day!

we are all eagerly awaiting the day when Ron Greenwood introduces an England Under-41 side!

Seriously, though, if enthusiasm is the key, the Commentators XI will be around for a few seasons yet. It may break a few more bones but we'll keep turning out on Sunday afternoons for as long as we can.

It's all made worthwhile for me by the words of one of our most distinguished 'guest' players, the Arsenal and England coach, Don Howe. 'To be honest,' Don told me, 'I've always been impressed by the standard of football the Commentators team manages to play. Normally in charity-type matches you get people chasing around for 20 minutes or so, then getting tired and the rest of the match becomes a bit of a joke.

'But the Commentators side treat it virtually as the pros would approach a game. You always try to play good, constructive football, you always want to win.

'It also adds a different dimension to your ability to commentate on the game. You can't beat being in the situation that you have to talk about week in and week out. When you're right there in the thick of things then you know the problems that the players are going through on a Saturday afternoon.'

So, the next time you hear an irate viewer criticising a commentator and muttering: 'What does he know about the game — he's probably never kicked a ball in his life . . .' you can be sure that he's certainly not talking about a *Match of the Day* man!

DID YOU KNOW?

Every time a Southend United player was booked during last season's Fourth Division promotion success, he paid a £10 fine. The money went into a large bottle and at the end of the season was donated to the leukaemia fund.

PERSONAL CHOICE

by Alan Parry

My team as a boy:
Liverpool . . . honestly! I was born in the city, started following them when they were still a Second Division club. My first favourite player was Alan A'Court, then Ian St. John (apologies to Bob Wilson!).

Career background:
Educated at Hillfoot Hey Grammar School, Liverpool. Joined local paper, the *Liverpool Weekly News,* as junior reporter, later moved to a freelance agency, *Mercury Press,* then the *Lancashire Evening Post & Chronicle.* Became sports editor, BBC Radio Merseyside, before joining BBC Radio Sport in 1972.

My first football assignment for BBCtv:
Easy to recall — my first commentary for *Match of the Day* was Manchester United v Leicester city on 13 September 1980. I'd joked with United manager Dave Sexton beforehand that perhaps he could arrange a few goals. He kept his promise — United won 5-0 . . . and we even had a dog on the pitch.

The ground with best facilities for TV coverage:
I think the Liverpool commentary position, just below the roof of the main stand, gives a perfect view and allows you to soak in the atmosphere. It's also warm and dry.

Other sports I have commentated on:
Many for radio, none for TV. My main 'second' sport is athletics and I've commentated on two Olympic Games — Montreal 1976, Moscow 1980.

Most memorable match I have covered:
For TV, last season's FA Cup-tie between Manchester City and Norwich. Man City won 6-0 and all the goals were spectacular.

Change in the game I would like to see:
The attitude of most clubs towards spectators. Directors should try watching from the terraces occasionally; it's so often darned uncomfortable, with poor catering and toilet facilities. Many grounds are difficult to get to and car-parking can be impossible for the fans.

Most exciting player in Britain today:
Glenn Hoddle has provided some great moments of excitement but for sheer ability and, more importantly, consistency, Kenny Dalglish is the player who gives me most pleasure.

The match I wish I could have covered:
The World Cup Final of 1966. It was one of those rare days in history when *everybody* remembers what they were doing . . .

Among my souvenirs:
I have a treasured collection of programmes and match tickets going back many years. But my favourite souvenir is a photograph taken when I *played* in front of 45,000 at Anfield on the night of Tommy Smith's testimonial. For me, that was a dream come true.

My biggest broadcasting gaff:
There have been plenty on radio. There was one freezing night at Manchester City when I was cursing the studio for keeping me hanging around. Unfortunately, the microphone was left on and every word, some of them real nasties, went out to the nation.

Manager I admire most:
It has to be Brian Clough. I don't always admire his methods but his achievements are second to none.

Funniest incident I've seen on a football field:
In a match between Leeds and Liverpool at Anfield, Gary Sprake, the Leeds goalkeeper, actually threw the ball into his own net, and within seconds the Kop was singing *Careless Hands.*

I'd give him a medal:
Every club secretary. He must be an organiser, financial wizard, public relations officer, psychologist, travel courier and 1001 other things, and often he doesn't even get to watch the games. What a job!

The man I would like to see manage England when Ron Greenwood retires:
Brian Clough's best quality is to make mostly average players blend into a formidable unit and that's not necessarily what is needed of an international manager. So my vote goes to Bobby Robson.

The man I think will get the job when Ron Greenwood retires:
Bobby Robson . . .

Aspect of the game that annoys me most:
People who earn a living from football but are constantly 'knocking' it.

1982 World Cup winners:
I think it could be one of the few tournaments where a South American country wins on European soil.

The Latin conditions in Spain will suit the Brazilians perfectly, and I expect the holders, Argentina, to do well again.

Alan Parry

PERSONAL CHOICE

'Does your mother come from Ireland?'

— or why the Republic of Ireland have such a good football team

by Desmond Lynam

Have you heard this Irish joke: 'When is an Irishman not an Irishman?' Answer: 'When he plays football for the Republic of Ireland'.

Since the FA of Ireland began to take full advantage of the rules governing qualifications for playing for one's country, that little yarn has become very familiar indeed. Some wags reckon the only qualification you need to turn out in a green jersey at Dalymount Park in Dublin is to know a couple of Irish jokes.

There's the story of Terry Mancini, born and mostly bred in London, a centre-half who spent all his playing career with London teams — Orient, Arsenal and QPR. With a name like Mancini, 'Henry' as he was affectionately known might not have been too surprised about a bit of Italian heritage. But late in his career an Irish granny was discovered in his cupboard and it wasn't long before 'Henry', cockney accent and all, found himself in the emerald green jersey, lined up for the pre-match preliminaries with the Republic about to take on the might of an Eastern European team.

The hand-shakes with the visiting dignitaries took place and then a hush fell over the ground as the band struck up. First one anthem, then another. Henry nudged the Dublin-born player by his side. 'Blimey', he said, 'which one's ours?'

In truth, if you were to look at any current 11 players that Republic of Ireland manager Eoin Hand might choose, half a dozen or so of them would have accents about as Irish as Yorkshire pudding.

Take this side: McDonagh, Langan, Hughton, O'Leary, Lawrenson, Daly, Grealish, Brady, Stapleton, Robinson and Heighway. Not a bad looking team . . . and a few players that the English FA would be delighted to get their hands on.

David O'Leary, Liam Brady and Frank Stapleton are proud possessors of a brogue as Irish as the Mountains of Mourne. Nothing sketchy about their national heritage. But Jim McDonagh was born in Yorkshire, Chris Hughton is a cockney sparrow from Battersea, Tony Grealish is also a Londoner, Mark Lawrenson and Steve Heighway have spent nearly all their lives in the north of England and Michael Robinson had not even been to Ireland until he played for them.

All of them, though, have either a parent or a grandparent born in the Republic and each is now the proud possessor of a little green book with a harp on the front of it — a Republic of Ireland passport.

Liam Brady, who last season proved his international quality by helping Juventus win the Italian League Championship, would walk into almost any national team. Stapleton and Robinson are a fine striking partnership, too, but the eyes of the English FA must look most enviously towards that top central defensive partnership which has given the Republic of Ireland team such a resolute back-bone — David O'Leary and Mark Lawrenson. There can't be many better pairings in world football

DID YOU KNOW?

When Stanley Matthews (now Sir Stanley) signed for Stoke City on his 17th birthday (1 February, 1932), the player who was to become one of the greatest wingers — and finest entertainers — in British football history was paid . . . one pound a week.

David O'Leary . . . the best centre-half in Britain 'by a street'.

and the FA of Ireland can thank Alan Kelly for it.

Kelly is a former Irish international and was a long-time servant of Preston North End FC.

Mark Lawrenson was born in Preston and signed for his local team on leaving school. He soon showed that he was going to be a very fine player and Alan Kelly became interested when he learned that Mark's mother had the soft Irish accent which he pinpointed as coming from the south-east of his native land. And, indeed, Mark's mother was born in County Waterford.

Kelly soon convinced the young player that, if he progressed, he could earn an Irish cap and was qualified so to do. Kelly tipped off the then Irish manager, Johnny Giles, and at the tender age of 18 Lawrenson found himself playing as an international, in a green shirt. As a boy he'd dreamed of playing for England but now he enthusiastically stepped out in the world football arena for Ireland.

Lawrenson was subsequently transferred to Brighton and Hove Albion, whose former manager, Alan Mullery, wishes that, for England's sake, Alan Kelly hadn't been quite so diligent.

Over the last couple of seasons Lawrenson has blossomed into one of the best central defenders in the First Division, although his club have mostly been at the wrong end of the table. He's received glowing praise for his performances from many of the top managers in the game and has become a highly valuable asset at Brighton.

Lawrenson considers David O'Leary to be the best centre-half in Britain 'by a street'. 'He's such a great reader of the game and deceptively quick, as so many First Division and international forwards find to their cost.

'Strangely, with his long legs and lengthy stride he doesn't look fast but whenever I've played with him my confidence has soared because he so rarely makes any kind of mistake.

'I think he has the sort of vision that Bobby Moore had but, in addition, he's so very good in the air. I've learned a great deal playing alongside him.'

O'Leary rates Lawrenson highly, too. 'He's a player who reminds me of Franz Beckenbauer. He's got vision and speed and

Mark Lawrenson . . . he displays the vision and speed of a Franz Beckenbauer.

also that skilful composure that enables him to go forward and create a dangerous situation for the opposition before they seem to catch on to what's happening.'

As an 'adopted' Irishman, Lawrenson receives a sackful of fan-mail from across the Irish Sea. "The fans seem knowledgeable and I like corresponding with them. They're also pretty well behaved and nowadays, because we're a match for almost any side, the interest in soccer seems to be growing.

'Of course "Anglos" like me and Michael [Robinson] take a lot of stick at our clubs for being picked for Ireland. But I can assure you that when we put on the green jerseys we're as proud as anyone and manager Eoin Hand has produced a wonderful spirit in the team. It's also run on very professional lines nowadays.

'In fact, if I'd been picked to play for an England team at 18 I might now be regretting that I'd forgotten that my mother came from Waterford and besides I wouldn't have David O'Leary to play alongside.'

Now, having been born of Irish parents myself, I've always had a soft spot for Irish football and I was just thinking the other day that it's a pity this fellow Maradona has already played for Argentina because I'm sure my Grandfather told me that there used to be a family of Maradonas down Limerick way.

FUNSPOT

FOLLOW YOUR LEADER

Find the answer to each question and take the first letter of his surname to spell the name of a world-famous soccer star.

1. Manchester United and Scotland striker.
2. Scored the 1978 FA Cup-winning goal.
3. His clubs have been Chelsea, QPR and Arsenal.
4. Liverpool and England defender.
5. Our star name's former international team-mate. Clue: they might sound double-Dutch.
6. Welshman who went to Canada via England.
7. Midlands star striker who cost £5,000.
8. Former Portuguese match-winner.
9. One of Ramsey's 1966 World Cup winners.

Answers on page 77

PERSONAL CHOICE

by Desmond Lynam

● **My team as a boy:**
Brighton & Hove Albion. Favourite players: Jimmy Langley, one of the best full-backs, and nicest of men, who ever drew breath: and Glen Wilson, a marvellous wing-half (midfield player) who has long served the club as trainer.

● **Career background:**
Born Ennis, Co. Clare, Republic of Ireland. Educated at Varndean Grammar School, Brighton. Began broadcasting in 1967 with BBC Local Radio; with Network Radio from 1969. Presenter of *Sports Report* and *Sport on 2;* BBC Radio boxing correspondent.

● **My first football assignment for BBCtv:**
Bristol City v Wolves, 1979-80. Match edited to four minutes, which resulted in a rather repetitive Lynam.

● **Club grounds with best facilities for TV coverage:**
Of those I have been to, Manchester City, Arsenal and Tottenham. All have good gantry positions and high, uncluttered view.

● **Other sports I have commentated on:**
Boxing for Radio and TV; tennis for Radio. I've presented programmes on virtually every sport.

● **Most memorable match I have covered on TV:**
Spurs v Leeds last season; I thought my commentary was bearable, the game was good and I met a man and his young son whose sight had been restored. They were so overjoyed to be able to see a game — something which I take for granted but now a little less so, having met them.

● **My kind of football reading:**
All major national newspapers. Pat Collins, of the London *New Standard,* impresses me with his knowledge, style and humour in his writing about the game.

● **Most exciting players in Britain today:**
I love style and especially players who can beat a man with the ball. Kevin O'Callaghan, who broke through in the Ipswich side last season, and Peter Barnes (WBA) excite me . . . so do Gary Shaw, of Aston Villa, and another Ipswich stylist, Frans Thijssen.

● **The match I wish I could have covered:**
England's World Cup victory in 1966. Not the greatest match, by any means, but certainly the greatest day for English football.

● **My biggest broadcasting gaff:**
'The ball's bobbling about between his legs!'

● **Among my souvenirs:**
A Brighton & Hove Albion club tie (but, then, I am one of their most committed fans and very biased).

● **Moment of magic I'll never forget:**
A brilliant goal by Peter Barnes for WBA against Leicester City. He ran from his own half, avoided several despairing tackles — and finished with a superbly struck swerving shot.

● **Managers I admire most:**
Alan Mullery, who brought so much into management when Brighton appointed him, and who lifted them from Third Division to First in three seasons. David Sexton — people forget he has taken two clubs within an ace of the League Championship (Manchester United and QPR). He is honest and a gentleman.

● **Personality of the past I would like to have interviewed:**
I already have — my boyhood idol, Tom Finney.

● **Oddest goal I've ever seen:**
Allan Hunter's own goal (Ipswich v Liverpool) — a superb swerver from near halfway. Bet he couldn't do it again.

● **I'd give him a medal:**
Me, for watching Brighton all through the lean years and being absolutely right about how great they would become. Roll on Europe and Wembley.

● **The man I would like to see manage England when Ron Greenwood retires:**
Clough or Mullery. Can't make up my mind. Success guaranteed either way (I think).

● **The man I think will get the job when Ron Greenwood retires:**
Bobby Robson.

● **I really rate:**
George Kerr, manager-character of Grimsby Town, who brought them from the Fourth Division so nearly to the First in successive seasons; West Ham, a club who have always been sensible and fair to their managers and players, especially when things have not been going so well. I've loved their FA Cup and promotion successes of the past two seasons.

● **1982 World Cup winners:**
West Germany, so difficult to beat in Europe. Brazil might do it, if they don't get kicked to pieces.

PERSONAL CHOICE

JOHN ROBERTSON, chunky, one-club Scottish International left-side attacker, has played a notable part in all Nottingham Forest's modern achievements. He arrived at the City Ground in March 1969 from Drumchapel Juniors, Glasgow, and starred in Forest's promotion team of 1977, their League Cup successes in 1978 and 1979 and European Cup triumphs in 1979 and 1980 (when he scored the winner against SV Hamburg). Sure-shot penalty-taker — 11 of his 12 goals last season were from the spot.

DAVID CROSS, of West Ham United, showed the finest form of his five-club career in season 1980-1. At 30, he scored 33 goals as West Ham stormed to the Second Division Championship and the League Cup Final. All this a year after earning an FA Cup winner's medal against Arsenal. Born at Bury, he began with Rochdale, moving to Norwich (October 1971 — £40,000), Coventry (November 1973 — £150,000) and WBA (November 1976 — £140,000) before West Ham paid £180,000 for him in December 1977.

SAMMY McILROY, of Manchester United, is an exciting midfield play-maker who followed the George Best trail from Belfast to Old Trafford to join United as an apprentice from school. His career blossomed from the start — he scored on his debut against local rivals, Manchester City, in November 1971, when only 17. He won his first cap three months later against Spain at Hull (Northern Ireland were not playing 'at home' at that time) and by the end of last season he had played in 50 full internationals.

DAI DAVIES, of Wrexham, 33-year-old Welsh-speaking goalkeeper, helped to give the Principality such a magnificent start in the qualifying stage of the 1982 World Cup. He made his international debut against Hungary in April 1975 and six years later (March 1981) equalled Wales' goalkeeper record of 41 caps by Jack Kelsey. Born at Ammanford, he began with Swansea, joined Everton (£25,000) in December 1970 and moved to Wrexham in September 1977. The fee of £8,000 made him one of the game's all-time bargains.

The 50-year gap

Tony Gubba selects his two most memorable personalities of last season — John Bond (here with Tottenham manager Keith Burkinshaw) and veteran goalkeeper Dick Pym (pictured overleaf). Their impact on football is half a century apart, but they are two men linked by a common love of the game. At the 100th FA Cup Final at Wembley in May they came within a few feet of each other, but never actually met. What a pity.

This man Bond

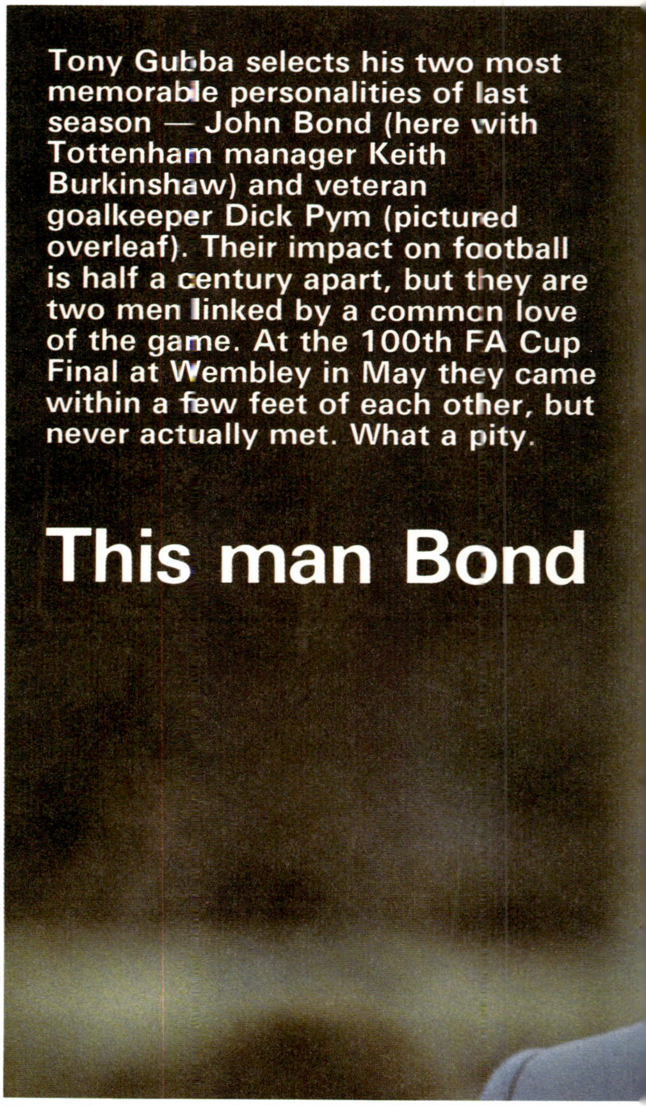

'AND LO, it shall come to pass', wrote the prophet, 'that from the East will come a new Messiah, wearing 300-guinea Savile Row suits and smoking wallet-thick cigars.

'And when all the tribe of Manchester City are in the depths of despair, he shall dock his ash on the pitch at Maine Road and all will be transformed. Yea, even as a miracle.

'And not even FA Cup Final defeat by the barbarians from Tottenham shall dull his glory.'

This is a loose translation from the ancient Mancunian scroll uncovered in October 1980 AD by the last Manchester City supporters tunnelling out of the locked ground.

Contrary to widespread belief, it was **not** found scribbled on the back of a discarded champagne bill.

Further translation of the historic text is hindered by heavy, dark stains, since chemically analysed as a mixture of blood, sweat and tears.

But, anyway, if you want to know more, it's easier to journey to Manchester and talk to the Messiah himself — John Bond.

The game of football has **never** witnessed a revival like that of Manchester City FC after John Bond was appointed their manager.

On the morning of Monday, 20 October 1980, when Bond accepted responsibility for the team, after watching the 1-0 home defeat by Birmingham on the Saturday, Manchester City stood bottom of the First Division with four points from 12 games. Relegation loomed as large as the shadow of the departing Malcolm Allison.

Seven months later, Bond's achievements at Maine Road had been little short of miraculous. Manchester City had finished the season in a healthy 12th place, been League Cup semi-finalists, and had been to Wembley to contest a memorable 100th FA Cup Final and replay against Tottenham Hotspur.

It's the price of success that someone will offer a reason why it isn't deserved.

John Bond himself will admit to being **almost** all the nasty things that critics have labelled him; flamboyant, outspoken, arrogant and deliberately controversial are among the less offensive. But Bond is also warm, enthusiastic, generous and a born self-publicist.

He does surround himself with the visible trappings of success. The crinkled scaled skin on his patent-shine shoes did once slither through some tropical swamp. And if the cut of cloth in a vast wardrobe of suits proclaims the highest bespoke tailoring, then the choice of colours reveals the man himself. It's all creams and light browns, nothing darkly conservative.

Already a dressing room legend is the tale of Bond's pre-Cup Final shopping for a new tie that ended with the purchase of £600 worth of clothing.

John Bond has always aimed big; big image, big cigar, big headlines, some might say big-headed. But, until the vacancy at Manchester City, never the cherished ambition of managing a big city club.

The prognosis wasn't good. Bond's first

bridged by football

verdict on Manchester City was 'a disaster'.

Although City had an overdraft of £1.6 million, the club pawned their last shreds of credibility to raise £750,000 and allow Bond to buy Phil Boyer (Southampton), Bobby McDonald (Coventry Reserves), Tommy Hutchison (also Coventry) and Gerry Gow (Bristol City).

This experience, added to the young legs of Nicky Reid, Tommy Caton, Ray Ranson, and Steve Mackenzie, became the cornerstone of City's remarkable transformation. The team took 20 points from the next 26 and that form, projected over the 42 games of the whole season, would have been good enough to win the League Championship with ease.

'Yea, even as a miracle,' had promised the Mancunian scroll.

It might even have added: 'So bright shall shine their glory, that the neighbouring kingdom of Old Trafford will be as if invisible in their shadow'.

Just before the Wembley replay, John Bond told me: 'There's a lovely grittiness about Northerners that I didn't fully appreciate until I moved to Maine Road. They're hungry for success. They want it — and they'll fight you for it. It's a terrific asset for a manager to have it in a team. There's no need to have to motivate people.'

It could be argued that Tottenham's stars needed the sharp realisation that, even in the

year of the cockerel, they could lose the Cup Final, before they were 'motivated' to try harder in the replay.

John Bond's football pedigree dates back to 1950 when he began his 17-year spell as a right back with West Ham, the last six of those years under manager Ron Greenwood. Despite being 6ft 2ins tall, over 12 stone, and nicknamed 'Muffin the Mule' by the Upton Park crowd, John Bond always favoured skilful rather than physical play.

As a young player, he was inclined to be truculent. When Ron Greenwood once complained at Bond's attitude to being dropped, and tried to soften the blow by explaining that he'd been dropped during his career too, Bond told him: 'Yes, but I'm a better player than you were'.

Greenwood later put Bond into West Ham's 'A' team and left him there for 18 months. Bond did play in West Ham's FA Cup-winning side against Preston in 1964 but subsequently moved on a free transfer to Torquay, where he completed his playing days.

After a brief coaching spell at Gillingham, Bond was appointed manager of Bournemouth in 1970 and in his first full season steered them to promotion into the Third Division. His side became the most attractive in the division, but they just failed to win promotion again.

Although Everton and Coventry tried to lure Bond from the Hampshire coast, it wasn't until Norwich City offered their vacant manager's seat that Bond was tempted into the deep waters of the First Division.

The Bond knack of making headlines often made him more newsworthy than the team. He achieved much at Norwich, despite severely limited resources. At Maine Road these days the bank manager needs a calculator to keep account of profits soaring to £750,000 from the League and FA Cup runs. From centre stage at Manchester City, the sky is the limit. So what next?

John Bond has never been over sensitive about weeding out players. Steve Daley's departure followed harsh, some say even tactless, criticism from Bond, who has made no secret either of his doubts about Dennis Tueart. And some of the stalwarts who salvaged City's season and pride will also have departed before long.

'I shall tell certain players "thank you, but your time is up" said Bond. 'It will make no difference whether or not I like the fellow. The job has to be done.'

Bond also adds: 'I won't have any bad apples. If a footballer is going to disrupt things, then it doesn't matter how much ability he's got, I won't have him.'

I am not a founder member of the John Bond Adoration Society. Indeed, there's a love of publicity in John Bond that may yet prove his Achilles heel. Teasing the tiger is all right until he turns and bites you and the ink in Fleet Street can run as lethal as hemlock. But, right now, let's give credit where credit is manifestly due.

It would be fascinating to look into the future via the ancient Mancunian scroll.

There is a section that begins: 'And after leading them from the wilderness . . .'

But then the text becomes obscured and confused and further translation is impossible.

Like Manchester City's impatient faithful, we shall have to wait and see.

This man Pym

THE CUP FINAL goalkeeper was seething with indignation. 'Their centre-forward', he exploded, 'kept standing on my toes at corners, trying to stop me jumping to catch the ball.

'But when I whacked him for it, the ref told **me** off.'

The goalkeeper's eyes shone with rage as anger blazed as fresh as when the incident happened — more than 50 years ago.

It was easy to forget that the man talking was now 88 years of age, and getting angry at the foul play of an opponent who has long since been dead.

When Dick Pym talks football, it's as if it were yesterday and not half a century ago.

Without any doubt, Dick Pym is the most fascinating and revealing personality I have ever met in football. He's a living, breathing part of the game's history. His sharp and lively mind can lift a unique corner of football's past. Never mind a million words in a thousand books, Dick Pym was actually there, playing the game. And he remembers it all.

Above the mantelpiece in Dick's small terraced home at Topsham, just outside Exeter, stands an oil painting of the man as he was in the 1920s — a fine figure in goalkeeper's green, shorts as full as sails and boots like suitcases.

Dick played in goal for Exeter between 1911 and 1921, was wounded in action in France in the First World War, then transferred to First Division Bolton for a record fee of £4,000.

Two years later he played in goal for Bolton in the first Wembley FA Cup Final against West Ham . . . and he went on to win **three** FA Cup-winners medals and never conceded a Wembley goal.

The record reads: 1923, Bolton 2, West

Wembley, 1923 . . . Goalkeeper Dick Pym in action for Bolton against West Ham.

Ham 0; 1926, Bolton 1, Manchester City 0; 1929, Bolton 2, Portsmouth 0.

Dick's wage for winning was £12.10s plus a gift of a watch, then a canteen of cutlery, and finally a grandfather clock that still ticks proudly in his home.

At the age of 32, Dick was selected for the first of his three international caps for England and he played First Division football until he was 38.

Despite the popular nostalgia for the 'good old days', when we are led to believe football was a fine, friendly game played by gentlemen, Dick recalls it all rather differently.

'There were quite a lot of ruffians in the game', he says. 'And a lot of them were boozing and gambling.

'Before every match at Bolton, a bottle of whisky was placed on the dressing room table. Players took a nip of it before going out to play. Anything left at full time was put into the tea. Some people took quite a long nip. But not me, I was teetotal.

'Those were the days of the dashing centre-forward,' recalls Dick. 'They would rush at a goalkeeper at full speed, trying to knock you over. You had to watch out of the corner of your eye.

'I remember a cup-tie against Blackburn in 1926 when their centre-forward, Bourton, made a mad rush at me as I jumped to catch a corner. He couldn't stop when I dodged out of the way and crashed into the goalpost, knocking himself unconscious.'

Dick never recollects receiving any coaching on how to play the game. 'We just went out each week and played,' he says. 'Our captain at Bolton in those days was a fellow called Joe Smith, a rough and ready sort of chap.

'One day the club chairman said he had a plan for our next match. Joe listened as he explained that at kick-off we should give the ball to our winger, he'd beat the full-back, cross the ball and our centre-forward would put it in the net to make the score 1-0.

'Joe then replied: "So then they kick off, give the ball to their winger, he beats our full-back, crosses and they score. 1-1. Why don't you .... off!

'The chairman never offered any more advice. But we must have been a reasonable side — we kept winning the FA Cup.'

At the 100th FA Cup Final celebrations at Wembley in May, Dick Pym was among the cavalcade of veteran Cup finalists introduced to the crowd before kick-off. No-one who has ever met Dick Pym could fail to be equally impressed by this marvellous old-timer whose love for the game, and memory of it, should be bottled like the elixir of life itself.

PERSONAL CHOICE

by Tony Gubba

● **My team as a boy:**
At school in Blackpool, I was too busy playing Rugby Union to watch Stanley Matthews and his illustrious counterparts. What a pity! Later, after moving back to Manchester, I watched the post-Munich United team — Quixall, Viollet, followed by Stiles, Setters, Law, Charlton and Best.

● **Career background:**
Born Moss Side, close to Manchester City's ground (1943), and went to Blackpool Grammar School (1955-60). Worked on *Sale Guardian, Lancashire Evening Telegraph* and *Daily Mirror* before going into TV with Southern Television at Southampton. Joined BBCtv as reporter in Liverpool in 1970.

● **My first football assignment for BBCtv:**
As a TV reporter in the North-West I went to Derby to interview Brian Clough on a bitterly cold January day. He put the camera crew in the boardroom and told us to help ourselves to the chairman's Scotch. 'He's very trusting,' I said. 'Don't think so,' said Brian. 'He marks the bottles.'

● **Club ground with best facilities for TV coverage:**
My occasional commentaries have taken me to only a dozen or so gantry positions. But the great pleasure in going to games in lower divisions is how well you are received.

● **Other sports I have commentated on:**
Ice-skating, speedway, table tennis, bobsleigh, ski-jumping, cross-country skiing, cycling, speed skating (that reminds me, I must ask the BBC for a rise!).

● **Most memorable match I have covered:**
Histon v Irthlingborough Diamonds — first match on the road to Wembley for the 100th FA Cup Final last season. Two little teams, a handful of people to watch and the game at true grass-roots level. More cows around than spectators . . . but still the same competition as that graced by Spurs, Liverpool etc. Ah, the magic of the Cup!

● **Changes in the game I would like to see:**
It doesn't seem so long ago that I was enjoying Manchester United, Chelsea and Tottenham in breathtaking games that ended 5-2, 4-3, 3-3. What happened? Where did they go? The success of teams like Don Revie's Leeds was the kiss of death for the days of free expression by highly talented individuals. Also, it's a dreadful indictment of society that we have to segregate rival supporters, ban booze at grounds and endure obscene chants and violence.

● **Most exciting players in Britain today:**
Only the two Dutchmen at Ipswich, Thijssen and Muhren, would force me to a match if my leg was in plaster and it was snowing. Perhaps Archibald, of Spurs, could prove equally attractive — if he continues to remind me of Greaves and Law.

● **The match I wish I could have covered:**
Any match in which Denis Law, Bobby Charlton and George Best played against Jimmy Greaves and Dave Mackay.

● **Among my souvenirs:**
A pair of ladies' tights! In the face of an icy wind blowing through an open-sided commentary box at the Scarborough v Crystal Palace third round FA Cup-tie in 1976, I found the only way to keep my legs and feet warm was to buy a pair and wear them beneath my trousers.

● **Moment of magic I'll never forget:**
Denis Law's debut for Manchester United was only ten minutes old when David Herd broke free on the right and crossed a high ball into West Brom's penalty-area. Law jumped . . . and for the first time the Stretford End saw that characteristic 'hang' in the air as he seemed to wait for the ball to arrive, then power it into the net.

● **Manager I admire most:**
One from long ago — Herbert Chapman. He was not only manager, but secretary as well, of Huddersfield and Arsenal when they won the League Championship three years in succession (Huddersfield in 1924-25-26, Arsenal in 1933-34-35).

● **Personality from the past I would like to have interviewed:**
Ellis Webb, who picked up the ball during a football match at Rugby School and created the game of rugby. Couldn't he play with his feet? Was it for a bet? Did he get thrashed — and if not, why not? Think of all the potential footballers subsequently lost to a rival game through his action.

● **The man I would like to see manage England when Ron Greenwood retires:**
Brian Clough. The only way we will ever know if he really is the greatest is by giving him *the* big job.

● **The man I think will get the job when Ron Greenwood retires:**
Bobby Robson.

● **1982 World Cup winners:**
West Germany.

Tony Gubba

PERSONAL CHOICE

PERSONAL CHOICE

from Scotland
by Archie Macpherson

● **My team as a boy:**
Airdrieonians, with Ian McMillan and Jimmy Welsh their stars.

● **My early days:**
Born Glasgow. Coatbridge High School. Jordanhill College.

● **My first football assignment for BBC tv:**
Hamilton Accies v East Fife. The Cuban Crisis was at its height. Kept my eye on the skies. Have been looking for missiles ever since. Commentary, unusually, was without mishap.

● **Club ground with best TV facilities in Scotland:**
Aberdeen. It's a Holiday Inn with a television platform.

● **Most memorable match I have covered:**
Holland v Scotland, Mendoza, World Cup 1978. Scotland won 3-2 but went out. As someone said: 'We discovered a new way of losing!'

● **My kind of football reading:**
All newspapers. Fond of that man from Kilmarnock who got a job writing on sport for *The Observer.* Hugh McIlvanney's the name — I never miss him.

● **Change in the game I would like to see:**
Nothing radical but it would be good to see clubs imposing harsh codes of discipline relating to behaviour on the field.

● **Most exciting player in Britain today:**
Andy Ritchie, of Morton. He defies the Laws of Gravity, perpetual motion and work rate . . . but entertains.

● **The match I wish I could have covered:**
England 1, Scotland 5 in 1928. The Wembley Wizards established the concept of annihilation.

● **Among my souvenirs:**
Helenio Herrera's autograph on the 1967 Inter-Milan v Celtic European Cup Final programme. Beside it are yellow smudges, which were his tear drops.

● **My biggest gaff, on-air:**
Why put it in print again, my lawyer says. My second biggest gaff was reversing the actual score during a Rangers-Celtic match three times in a row. I went ex-directory next day.

● **Moments of magic I'll never forget:**
Archie Gemmill's goal against Holland in Mendoza (World Cup '78). Bobby Charlton scoring with a 25-yarder on his England debut — against Scotland at Hampden, 1958.

● **Manager I admire most:**
Jock Stein. When you win a European Cup and create a whole new domestic style, you are unique.

● **Personality of the past I would like to have interviewed:**
Greta Garbo. Failing that, Sir Stanley Matthews. On the football field he did a lot of harm to the Scots but some of his biggest admirers were north of the border.

● **Funniest goal I've ever seen:**
John Motson scoring a 30-yarder that touched the underside of the bar on its way to bulging the net in a bounce game with Scottish Press and TV in Norway in 1974. It was an own goal.

● **I'd give him a medal:**
The cameraman on a 30ft platform leaning into a 90-mile sou'wester while still managing to spot the ball.

● **Wishing on a star:**
I know it's a pie in the sky but it would be interesting to see what effect it would have on the game in Scotland, or indeed England, if our talent could be kept our side of the border, so that we could develop our own game untouched. As far as young Scottish talent and English scouts go, all Scottish families should adopt that old prayer: 'Lord, save us from the Vikings!'

● **1982 World Cup winners:**
West Germany. They know what winning is all about and draw on a very deep and broad pool of players. They own half of Spain anyway.

PERSONAL CHOICE

FUNSPOT - ANSWERS

Nickname Know-How — *page 8.*

Answers:

1. TOFFEES (Everton)
2. KILLIES (Kilmarnock)
3. BLADES (Sheffield United)
4. MARINERS (Grimsby)
5. GUNNERS (Arsenal)
6. BULLY WEE (Clyde)
7. CHERRIES (Bournemouth)
8. PILGRIMS (Plymouth Argyle)
9. EAGLES (Crystal Palace)
10. BEES (Brentford)
11. RAILWAYMEN (Crewe)
12. SPURS (Tottenham)
13. RAMS (Derby)
14. TROTTERS (Bolton)
15. GERS (Rangers)
16. IMPS (Lincoln City)
17. HATTERS (Luton Town)
18. STAGS (Mansfield)
19. POSH (Peterborough)
20. SWANS (Swansea City)
21. GRECIANS (Exeter City)
22. SHAKERS (Bury)
23. QUAKERS (Darlington)
24. CANARIES (Norwich City)
25. SADDLERS (Walsall)

Dial-a-Star — *page 18.*

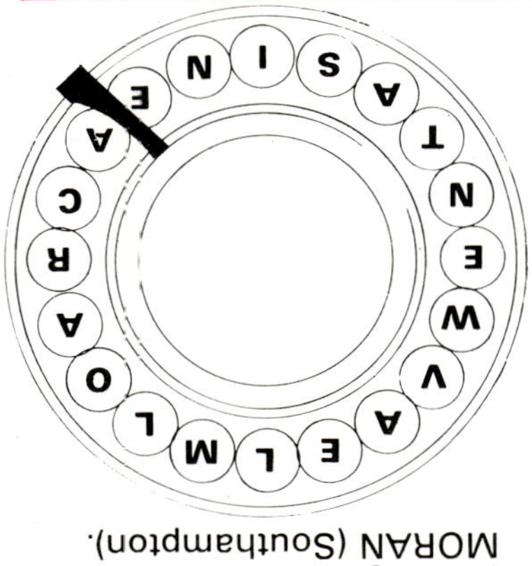

Answers: IAN WALLACE (Nottingham Forest), STEVE MORAN (Southampton).

Today's Clubs — Long Ago — *page 32.*

Answers: 1. QPR v Oldham; 2. Plymouth Argyle v Manchester United; 3. Bristol Rovers v Bristol City; 4. Birmingham v Coventry City; 5. Gillingham v Manchester City; 6. Stockport County v Cambridge United.

Crossword Solution — page 25

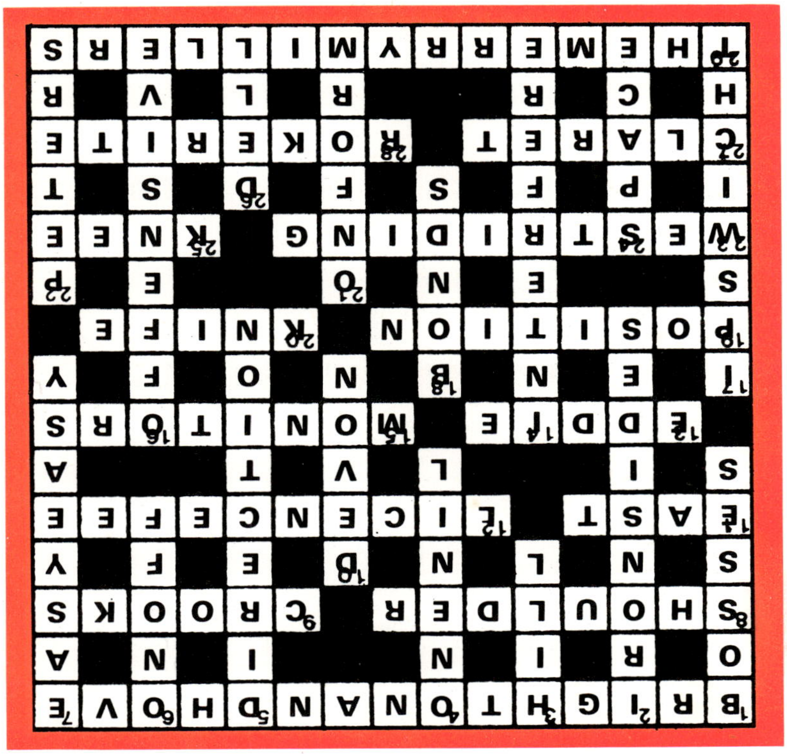

Spot the Teams — *page 51.*

Answers:

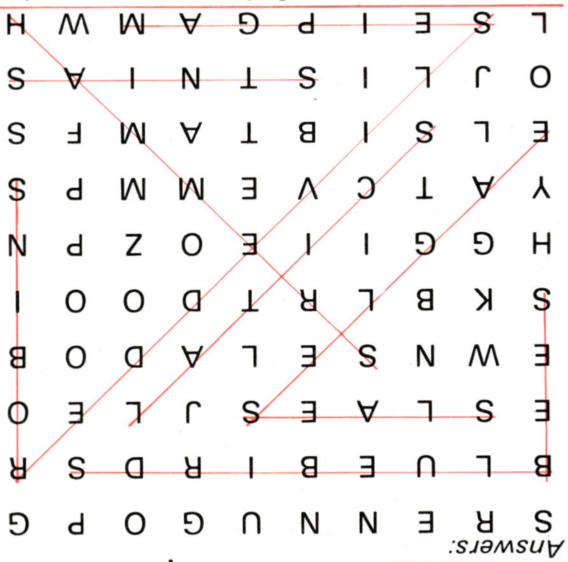

Whose is the Badge? — *page 59.*

Answers:

1. Charlton,
2. Ipswich,
3. Leicester,
4. Mansfield,
5. Bristol City,
6. Grimsby,
7. Sheffield Wednesday,
8. Rotherham,
9. Port Vale,
10. Newcastle.

Follow Your Leader — *page 64.*

Answers:

1. Jordan, 2. Osborne, 3. Hollins, 4. Neal, 5. Neeskens, 6. Yorath, 7. Regis, 8. Eusebio, 9. Peters. World star — Johnny Rep.

Moore the Merrier — *page 45*

Answers:

1. 1923 — 15
2. 1958 — 23
3. 1974 — 21
4. 1979 — 26
5. 1976 — 23

Total: 108

It's good in't it?

World Cup action . . . 6 June 1981, Budapest: England captain Kevin Keegan drives his penalty shot wide of Hungary's diving goalkeeper to complete England's 3-1 World Cup qualifying match victory. It was a vital win. A week earlier England had crashed to defeat against Switzerland. Victory for Hungary would have ended English hopes of qualifying for the 1982 World Cup Finals in Spain. But Ron Greenwood picked his team for 'character and commitment' — and England's players produced a performance that matched his highest hopes. The road to World Cup glory was open again . . .

Acknowledgements
All Sport 40, 49
Bob Thomas 2, 4, 5, 6, 8, 10, 13, 27, 28, 38, 40, 52, 53, 66, 67
BBC Hulton Picture Library 74
Camera Press 5
Colorsport 11, 12, 22, 26, 37, 40, 44, 55, 63, 64
Don Smith 16
George Herringshaw 20, 21, 45, 68
Jeremy Grayson 73
Mike Davidson 17
Sporting Pictures 5, 21, 23, 29, 34, 36, 40, 54, 70
Syndication International 25
Terry Rand 56

Published by the British Broadcasting Corporation, 35 Marylebone High Street, London W1M 4AA
ISBN 0 563 17948 1
First published 1981

Printed by Severn Valley Press